D1029588

WALLS

African American Life Series

*A complete listing of the books in this series
can be found at the back of this volume.*

General Editors

Toni Cade Bambara
Author and Filmmaker

Wilbur C. Rich
Wayne State University

Geneva Smitherman
Michigan State University

Ronald W. Walters
Howard University

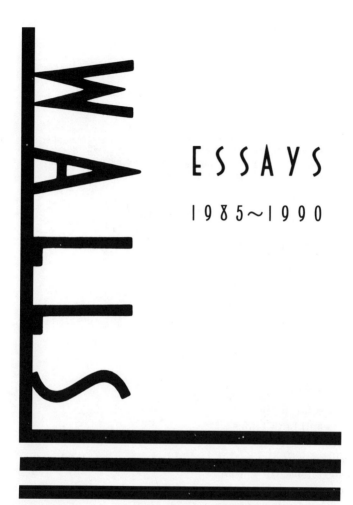

WALLS

ESSAYS

1985~1990

Kenneth A. McClane

 Wayne State University Press   Detroit

95 94 93 92 91   5 4 3 2 1

Library of Congress Cataloging-in-Publication Data
McClane, Kenneth A., 1951-
    Walls: essays, 1985–1990 / Kenneth A. McClane.
        p. cm. — (African American life series)
    ISBN 0-8143-2134-8 (alk. paper)
    1. Afro-Americans—Social conditions—1975-
    2. Afro-Americans—Biography. I. Title. II. Series.
E185.86.M387 1991
305.896'073—dc20   90-22624

Designer: Mary Krzewinski

Other books by Kenneth A. McClane

Out Beyond the Bay
Moons and Low Times
To Hear the River
At Winter's End
These Halves Are Whole
A Tree Beyond Telling: Selected Poems
Take Five: Collected Poems, 1971–1986

For Alvin Aubert

Who knows but that, on the lower frequencies,
I speak for you?

—Ralph Ellison, *Invisible Man*

Contents

Acknowledgments 11

Introduction 13

A Death in the Family 17

Walls: A Journey to Auburn 29

The School 45

Unity Day 65

Baxter's Program:
Creative Writing at Cornell 77

Intimate Injustice 83

Keep On Keeping On 97

Between Yes and No 111

Acknowledgments

I would like to thank the editors of the following magazines in which some of these essays first appeared: *The Arts and Sciences Newsletter* for "Baxter's Program"; *Community Review* for "Walls: A Journey to Auburn"; *Epoch* for "Unity Day"; *Northwest Review* for "The School" and "Keep On Keeping On"; and *River Styx* for "Intimate Injustice."

"A Death in the Family," © The Antioch Review, Inc., first appeared in *Antioch Review*, vol. 43, no. 2, Spring 1985. Reprinted by permission of the Editors.

I would also like to thank Robert Atwan and Annie Dillard for reprinting my essay "Walls: A Journey to Auburn" in *The Best American Essays 1988* (Ticknor and Fields, 1988).

"A Death in the Family" was reprinted in *The Black Scholar* in 1987.

I would especially like to thank Kathryn Wildfong for her invaluable assistance.

Introduction

The essays that make up this collection are largely personal ones, which means that I have the freedom and the responsibility to be both self-absorbed and self-corrective. Clearly, the truths I narrate are largely my own: no one can maintain that this or that did not happen unless they were there. And yet, by the same token, I have the awesome responsibility to protect those who were present—since events did occur, and I am not the only person to have been directly influenced by them. That these "silent" people did not have a hand in the actual writing of this—indeed, that some of them are now dead—means that I have an even more Herculean obligation to tell it well. If I somehow managed here not to break faith with myself, I hope that I have never consciously broken faith with others.

The first essay in this book, "A Death in the Family," began one morning while I was remembering my brother Paul. Paul died of alcoholism in 1983, and I, from that moment on, undertook the long process of grieving, one which would tell me a great deal not only about my dead brother but about myself. In truth, Paul's death, paradoxically, made my life *real.*

So early one morning I began writing my first essay. It was a difficult process. As a poet, I had always shied away from prose: sentences terrified me. Indeed, I became a poet in the 1960s largely because I felt that my rhythms were undisciplined and jagged; the poem seemed the logical place for my wanderings. Until that Sunday morning—when I began to write feverishly with tears in my eyes—I had remained a poet, happily, for six books.

But Paul's death—and its terrible pain—caused me to become self-infested. I wanted to cry, shout, flail; I wanted to embrace pain, to coddle it, to finger every inch of my loss. If poems could do this, I did not know how, and so I began to write "A Death in the Family" in 1985. It was my first essay; there would be others.

Still, I am a poet by training and yearning, and these essays are "poetic" ones. By "poetic" I mean that they follow a poet's logic, using the heartfelt, the passionate, and the rhythmic to urge their announcements. If I could not have employed this form, I would not have written. And I *needed* to write. Writers scribble not only to convey something; they write to live. As a Chinese proverb states, "A bird does not sing because he has the answer. He sings because he has a song."

If my brother Paul is the symbolic hub of this collection, his presence is made manifest in different ways throughout the essays. At times he is the sole impetus for a piece, as in "A Death in the Family" and "Unity Day." At other times he is a distant oracle. In every essay, Paul is the constant harbinger of the significance of the fleeting, the present, the changeable. If I have learned anything, it is that death is irrefutable; no one, I would argue, understands time until he has lost someone irretrievably. Paul's death, most certainly, taught me the importance of witness, of seeing. These essays are one person's testimony to the wonderment of life.

Not all of these essays concern my brother; some of them do not even mention my family. One involves a trip to an upstate maximum-security prison; another, a fleeting meeting with the great writer James Baldwin; still another, a reminiscence about Baxter Hathaway, my first creative writing teacher, and his excellent writing program at Cornell. All, I hope, are trenchant and honest.

A number of these essays have appeared elsewhere, and I am most thankful to the editors. "Walls: A Journey to Auburn" (first published in *Community Review*) was included in *The Best American Essays 1988*, edited by Robert Atwan and Annie Dillard. "Unity Day" was first published in *Epoch;* "The School" in *Northwest Review;* "A Death in the Family" in *Antioch Review;* and "Baxter's Program" in the *Arts and Sciences Newsletter.*

Yet what most pleases me is that these essays have found their way into Alcoholics Anonymous workshops, prison programs, and university lecture halls. This, at least, suggests that I may have gotten something right. If I have been indelicate, I hope my dereliction from human sensitivity and craft has been short term. If these essays are ugly, I only wish that I had written better. If they are dishonest, then please hold me responsible, for the people and the experiences I labored to capture were wondrous; they are certainly worthy of the masterful.

I must thank Wayne State University Press for being so patient with me, especially as I procrastinated and worried myself and others threadbare; my wife, Rochelle, for keeping me whole; my parents and sister for loving me; and Alvin Aubert—editor, poet, critic, and friend—to whom I dedicate this volume, and to whom many young writers owe more than words can convey.

I hope my temporary sojourn with the essay is a propitious one. The pieces collected here were written between 1985 and 1990. I wince at the occasional ugliness of the prose. I cringe when I know that, however much I tried, my wonderful sister has remained largely unknown to me.

Every writer wishes that he or she wrote better. I, for one, am thankful that the essay, however failed my execution, presented me with the gift of form. I can never have my brother back, and yet the love I now understand—the love gleaned in this meek testimony—argues for a world that is irrefutably provident.

I once wrote in a poem, "Always this wintry world wanders from the knife to the cross." And so it does. My brother is dead; I am here. It is laid to me to make his passing of note; as it is laid to all of us to value in others what we prize in ourselves.

When I left for college in 1969, my brother wished me "Godspeed." He was excited for me; he was also happy to see me go, since now the bedroom would all be his. Yet I remember how strange it was to be saying good-bye to him—stranger, indeed, that he would use the Lord's name in his parting statement. Paul had never been religious; he was certainly not one for prayer. And yet this moment truly was sanctified: I was going away from home to become what I might; Paul was remaining, trying to finish his last two years of high school, before he went out into the world. Neither of us knew what the ensuing ten years would bring, in happiness or tragedy. Neither of us, I submit, wanted to broach the subject.

When I think of that day, and all the life and the death it concealed, I want to wish Godspeed to everyone.

K. M.
March 22, 1990
Ithaca, New York

A Death in the Family

> He was a kid of about the same age as Rufus, from
> some insane place like Jersey City or Syracuse, but
> somewhere along the line he had discovered that he
> could say it with a saxophone. He had a lot to say.
> He stood there, wide-legged, humping the air,
> filling his barrel chest, shivering in the rags of his
> twenty-odd years, and screaming through the horn
> *Do you love me? Do you love? Do you me?* And,
> again, *Do you love me? Do you love me? Do you
> love me?*
>
> —James Baldwin, *Another Country*

I recall how difficult it was for me to realize that my brother loved me. He was always in the streets, doing this and that, proverbially in trouble, in a place, Harlem, where trouble indeed was great. At times we would even come to blows, when, for example, drunk as he could be, he wished to borrow my car and I had visions of his entrails splayed over the city. I remember one incident as if it were yesterday: Paul, my younger brother, physically larger than me, his hand holding a screwdriver, poised to stab me, his anger so great that his brother, the college professor, wouldn't let him drive his "lady" home, even though he could barely walk. I can still see him chiding me about how I had always done the right thing, how I was not his father, how I was just a poor excuse for a white man, the last statement jeweled with venom. And from his place, this was certainly true: I had done what I was expected to do; and the world, in its dubious logic, had paid me well. I was a college teacher; I had

17

published a few collections of poems; I had a wonderful girl-friend; and what suffering I bore, at least to my brother's eyes, centered around my inability to leave him alone. Luckily, this confrontation ended when my father rushed in on us, our distress exceeded only by the distress in his eyes. Later, my brother would forget the events of that evening, but not the fact that I had not lent him the car. For my part, I would never forget how we were both so angry, so hate-filled. I, too, that night, might have killed my brother.

As children we were often at each other's throat. The difference in our ages, just two years, was probably a greater bridge than either of us welcomed. And so we often went for each other's pressure points: the greater discomfort enacted, the more skillful our thrust. But this was child's play, in a child's world. On that November night when my brother and I confronted each other with hate and murder in our eyes, I realized I had mined a new intensity, full of terror and, though I didn't know it then, of love.

Though he was incredibly angry (bitter, some might say), I always admired my brother's honesty and self-love. It seemed that everything he thrust into his body was a denial of self—alcohol, smoke, cocaine—yet his mind and his quick tongue demanded that he be heard. In a world full of weakness, he was outspoken, never letting anyone diminish him. When he was at the wheel of that torturous abandon euphemistically called "city driving," he invariably would maneuver abreast of a driver who had somehow slighted him, and tell him, in no uncertain language, where he could go and with utmost dispatch. Paul never cared how big, crazy, or dangerous this other driver might be. When I cautioned him, reliving again and again the thousand headlines of "Maniac Kills Two over Words," he would just shrug. "He's a bastard, needs to know it." I remember how scared I became when he would roll down the window—scared and yet proud.

My brother was unable to ride within the subway, moving immediately to the small catwalk between the cars, where the air might reach him. He complained that he was always too hot, that the people were too close; indeed, as soon as he entered the train, sweat began to cascade off him, as if he had just completed a marathon. Later this image would remain with me: my brother, feet apart, sweat pouring from his body, trying to keep his delicate balance between the two radically shifting platforms, while always maintaining that he was fine. "Bro, I'm just hot." I would later learn that these manifestations were the effects of acute alcoholism; I would later learn much about my brother.

Like the day's punctuation, Paul would make his numerous runs to the *bodega,* bringing in his small brown paper bags, then quickly returning to his room, where he would remain for hours. Some days you would barely see him; my father could never coax him out. Paul saw my father as the establishment— "fat man," he would call him, though this too was somewhat playful. With Paul play and truth were so intermeshed that they leased the same root. One had to be forever careful of traveling with a joke only to find that no joke was intended. Or, just as often, finding sympathy with something Paul said, one was startled to see him break out in the most wondrous smile, amusement everywhere. In this spectacle, one thing was enormously clear: Paul was a difficult dancer. And, as with all artists, his mastery was also, for the rest of us, cause for contempt. We enjoyed his flights; but we also sensed, and poignantly, that they were had at our expense. Clearly we had failed as listeners, for Paul had not sought to befuddle us; but we, as the majority, were in the position of power and could always depend on it as our last defense. And power, arguments to the contrary, is rarely generous.

My brother would stay in his room for hours, watching the box, playing his drums, talking to his endless friends who, until he was just about to die, came to sit and talk and smoke. Paul inevitably would be holding court; he knew where the parties were, could get anyone near anything, had entrée with the most beautiful girls, who sensed something in his eyes that would not betray them. Many of his friends would later become doctors, a few entertainers, all of them by the most incomprehensible and torturous of routes. The black middle class—if it can really be termed that—is a class made up of those who are either just too doggedly persistent or too stupid to realize that, like Fitzgerald's America, their long-sought-after future remains forever beckoning and endlessly retreating. And Paul's friends, who sensed his demise well before we did, as only the doomed or the near-doomed can, were as oddly grafted to class—or even the promise of respectability—as it is humanly possible to imagine. Like Paul, they sat waiting for the warden, knowing only that the walls exist, that the sentence is real. Indeed, if the crime were lack of understandable passion, they were guilty a hundredfold. But it is not understanding, alas, that the world is interested in. And the world—they rightfully sensed—was certainly not interested in them.

Paul was no saint. Like most of us, he exhibited the confusions and the possibilities that intermittently set us on our knees or loose with joy. He wasn't political in the established way; his body, in its remoteness, was political. It said that the state of the world was nothing he cared to be involved with. Fuck it, he'd say.

In the language of the street, Paul was a "lover." And like all lovers he believed that the pounding of the bed frame testified to something that "his woman" best understood. And in the logic of his bed and of those who shared it, women's lib to the contrary, there seemed to be no complaints. Often I wondered about his use of the term "my woman," the possessiveness of it, the language that brought to mind the auction block and a brutal history that had profited neither of us. But Paul's woman was like his life: if I had my job and my poems, he had his woman. Feminists might complain of this uneasy pairing—I certainly share their concern—but within the brutal reward structure of the ghetto, where one's life is often one's only triumph, such a notion is understandable. My brother's woman was his only bouquet, the one thing that testified that he was not only a man, but a man whom someone wanted. Arguments notwithstanding, no manner of philosophy or word play can alter the truth. My brother loved his woman in the most profound sense of the word, since his love centered on the greatest offering he could give, the sharing of himself. And I do not mean to be coy here. For when you are, in Gwendolyn Brooks's terms, "all your value and all your art," the gift of yourself is an unprecedented one.

But this is a brother's testimony; it is a way of a brother living with a brother dead. It doesn't have the violence of unknowing—the great violence that kept me for so long feeling guilty, which still makes the early morning the most difficult time. I remember how Paul volunteered to watch our cats when Rochelle and I, living for a three-month exile in Hartsdale, New York, had to be away. Max, the large white one, hell-bent on intercourse with the hardly possible, hid within the wall, and Paul went nearly crazy, looking here and there, wondering if he should call, afraid that disaster had no shores. Strange how I recall this; it certainly isn't important. But Paul was scared— scared more so because he loved animals, saw in their pain more than he saw in ours, in his.

In July, my father called to say that I had best come to New York. Paul was ill. Very ill. He would probably die. The whole thing was incredible. My father has the nagging desire to protect those he loves from the worrisome. What this tends to create, however, is the strangest presentiment: when he does finally communicate something, it is always at the most dire stage, and the onlooker can barely understand how something has become so involved, so horrible, so quickly; or is thrown, similarly, into the uncomfortable position of confronting the possibility that one failed to acknowledge something so momentous occurring. In either case, one is completely unprepared for revelation, and no matter what my father's heroic designs (and they were that), one's horror at not being allowed to participate in the inexorable outdistances any possible feeling of gratitude. Although pain cannot be prepared for, neither can it be denied. But on this day, my father's voice was that of cold disbelief—the doctor without any possible placebo. And I was in the air in a few hours.

At that time I was involved in teaching summer school, and the day before one of my students had suggested that we read Baldwin's *Sonny's Blues*. I had read the story some years before and had been favorably impressed, though I couldn't remember any of its particulars. Well, at six-fifteen I got on the airplane, armed with a few clothes and Baldwin. Little did I know that this story would save my life, or at least make it possible to live with it.

Sonny's Blues is about an older brother's relationship with his younger brother, Sonny, who happens to be a wonderful jazz pianist and a heroin addict. The story, obviously, is about much more: it involves love, denial, and the interesting paradox by which those of us who persist in the world may in fact survive, not because we understand anything but because we consciously exclude things. Sonny's older brother teaches algebra in a Harlem high school, where algebra is certainly not the only education the students are receiving. There are drugs, dangers, people as hell-bent on living as they are fervent on dying. But most importantly, *Sonny's Blues* is about the ways in which we all fail; the truth that love itself cannot save someone; the realization that there are unreconcilable crises in the world; and, most importantly, the verity that there are people among us, loved ones, who, no matter what one may do, will perish.

Now, I read this story on the plane, conscious, as one is only when truly present at one's distress, of the millions of things going on about me. The plane was headed to Rochester, a course only capitalism can explain, for Rochester is west of Ithaca; and New York, my destination, is east of Ithaca, my place of origin. Clearly this makes no sense, but neither does serving gin and tonic at six-fifteen A.M. And I was thankful for that.

The hospital was located in central Manhattan, some five blocks from my father's newly acquired office. My father had just moved from his long-held office at 145th Street because he had routinely been robbed; the most recent robbery had taken on a particularly brutal nature, when the intruders placed a huge, eight-hundred-pound EKG machine atop him to pin him to the floor. Robberies in this neighborhood were not unusual; my father had been robbed some eight times within the previous four years. But with the escalation of the dope traffic, and the sense that every doctor must have a wonderful stash, doctors, even when they, like my father, had no narcotics at all, became prime targets. My father loved his office; he had been there since he first came to New York in 1941. Although he could have made much more money in Midtown, he remained by choice in Harlem. As a child I could not understand this. I wanted him to be among the skyscrapers, with the Ben Caseys. Little did I know then that his forsaking all these things was the highest act of selflessness. As he once quietly stated, probably after a bout of my pestering, "Black people need good doctors, too." I imagine my father would have remained in his office until a bullet found his head had not my mother finally put her foot down and declared, "Honey, I know thirty-five years is a long time, but you've got to move."

I walked past my father's new office and headed into the intensive care unit of Roosevelt Hospital. There I met my father and the attending physician—two doctors, one with a son—and listened to the prognosis. Medicine, as you know, has wonderful nomenclature for things: the most horrible things and something as slight as hiccups have names that imply the morgue. But the litany of my brother—septicemia, pneumonia— had the weight, rehearsed in my father's face, of the irreconcilable. My brother was *going* to die. The doctor said my brother was *going to die.* They would try like hell, but the parameters (the word *parameters* had never before been so important to me) left little in the way of hope.

It is difficult enough to be a parent and have a twenty-nine-year-old child dying of alcoholism, his gut enlarged, his eyes red, lying in a coma. It is even more difficult, however, when you are a parent and also a doctor. For you have a dual obligation, one to a profession, a way of seeing, and one to

23

nature, a rite of loving. As a doctor, my father knew what was medically possible—as surely as did any well-trained special-ist—in my brother's precarious situation; he certainly knew what the parameters dictated. But as a parent, hoping like any parent that his child might live, he knew nothing, hope being a flight from what is known to the fanciful. And so these two extremes placed my father in a country rarely encountered, a predicament where I could sense, even then, his distress, but a place from which no one could save him.

In the two weeks that would follow, my mother, in grief, would ask my father what were Paul's chances. And he—doctor, parent, and husband—would be placed in that country again and again. As a parent, every slight twitching of Paul, a slight movement of the lips, a small spasm of the hand, would move him to joy, to speculation—was that an attempt at words, was Paul reaching out? But as a doctor, he knew the terrible weight of parameters—how a word, no matter how strange its sound or source, does involve meaning. So, often he was placed in the terrible paradox of stating what he least wanted to hear. That yes, it was possible that Paul was reaching for us; but the parameters, the this test and the that test, suggested that Paul was still critical, very critical. And we never pressed him fur-ther, probably sensing that he would have to announce that these small skirmishes with the inevitable, like water pools just before turning to ice, could not remove the fact, no matter how much we or he would wish it so, that Paul was going to die. Moreover, for us, this dalliance with hope was a temporary way station so that we could harden our own tools for the coming onslaught. My father did not have this privilege; he was, like all the greatest heroes, the angel without the hope of heaven.

In many ways the third factor in my father's difficult situation now came most into play: that of husband. My mother, like all of us, clung to hope; but more, she clung to her son. There is no way to detail the sense of a mother's love. In substance, a mother protects her son from the world, which, she rightly senses, is unceasingly bent on his destruction. Yet, in my house, since Paul was an artist—and so remote—my mother, in a sense, defended a phantom, defending him in much the way one supports the constitutional right of due process. For my mother, Paul was to be protected in theory: he was an artist; he was sensitive; he was silent. This identification with him and with those of his facets the world was bound not to respect—and indeed never did—made her involvement with Paul all the more intense, for he was not only the issue of her womb but the wellspring of her imagination.

My father certainly understood some of this, yet his way of reacting to any ostensible conundrum was conditioned by his medical school training. If there was a problem, he maintained, it could be reasonably addressed. And so he hoped that Paul would descend from his room and tell him what the problem was, why he wasn't finishing college, why he continued to drink so heavily, what, in God's name, he did up in that room. And as it became obvious that the Socratic method demanded an interchange between two consenting mentors, my father became increasingly concerned and distressed. (The problem with any axiom is that it is valuable only as long as it works: my father's belief in reason had served him happily heretofore; yet now he was encountering an unforeseen circumstance. And he, like all of us when confronting Paul, had little in the bank.)

In any event, my father, in the hospital, was forced continually to grapple with three very difficult responsibilities all somehow connected. My mother, as Paul miraculously showed slight signs of rallying (the doctors had originally stated that he had a ten-percent chance of surviving), continued to find reasons, as all of us did, for hope. I recall how my wife and I visited one day and Paul actually extended his wobbling hand—and I, relating this later to my father, actually did press him, asking him if he thought Paul could possibly make it. My father, caught between a brother's hope and the sense that miracles do

25

happen, and possibly even to him, said, "Yes, I think he could; but the parameters (*again that word*) are inconclusive." (Now I know that he didn't believe that Paul could live—the doctor in him didn't believe, that is.)

But the most difficult moments for my father came, I think, when he had to explain to my mother, his wife, what he saw, trying always to remember that she was a grieving mother and a hopeful one; and no matter what was happening, might happen, he had to remain a source of strength for her, as she had so often been for him. In this difficult barter, my father also had to worry about my mother's natural inclination to believe the impossible, for hope would make us all immortal, while at the same time protecting that part of her which would permit her to bear this thing, no matter what the outcome. My father continued to caution my mother about the dire state of my brother. The word *parameter* became as palpable to my family as my brother's breath. And the boundaries, no matter what my brother's outward appearance, remained the same. It was enough to drive one crazy. With the weather, when the sun rises and the skin feels warm, the thermometer registers one's sense of new heat. Yet with my brother it seemed that our senses were at war with the medical reality. What, then, in this place, were cause and effect?

During the last week of my brother's life, my mother became increasingly angry with my father, blurting out, "You sound as if you want your son to die." Clearly this was an outburst culled out of anguish, frustration, and grief. And yet it adequately gave language to my father's paradox. Never have I seen the mind and the heart so irrefutably at odds.

My brother died after five coronaries at two A.M. thirteen nights after he was admitted to intensive care. His funeral took place some 250 miles from New York, on lovely Martha's Vineyard, where Paul and the family had spent our happiest years. The funeral was a thrown-together affair: 90 percent grief and the rest dogged persistence that something had to be done. The service was a plain one, with an Episcopal minister reading from the dreary Book of Common Prayer. My mother had hoped that someone could better eulogize my brother, someone who might get beyond the ashes-to-ashes bit and talk about the stuff of him, possibly so that we, his family, might finally get to know the person who had slowly drained away from us. The one reverend who knew my brother begged off, with the excuse that Paul had traveled a great distance from when he knew him. And that, to say the least, was the profoundest ministry that man had ever preached.

Although the funeral was a hasty affair, with little notice—and though we hardly knew many of Paul's friends—somehow a large contingent gathered, coming from Vermont, New York, and elsewhere, many of them for the first time at a funeral of one of their peers. I can't adequately describe the motley assemblage. Suffice it to say that these were the Lord's children, the ones who had tasted the bread of this world and waited, still, for manna. One young woman said a few words, choked them out, and then the sobbing began.

I think this meditation aptly ends with his friends, for they knew him and loved him as we did. In Baldwin's *Another Country*, one of the characters, Vivaldo, is described as feeling that "love is a country he knew nothing about." With the death of my brother, I learned about love: my love for him; my love for my parents; their love for each other; my love for those thin-shelled children who gathered on that small hillside to pay witness to one of theirs who didn't make it, who evidenced in his falling that death indeed is a possibility, no matter how young one is or how vigorous. I can't say that I know who my brother was, but I know that I miss him, more now than ever. And love, yes, is a country I know something about.

Walls: A Journey to Auburn

Paul

The willows are gold again
and now the season seems past thinking
seems past remembrance, seems past
the long lean taking of your breath:

I remember you Paul, always, how you strutted
among the city—Lord of the manor; how you
fought with the drivers, how you never
let one person call you *nigger*. I remember how

you struggled with Dad—loving him in the stridency
of your ill-conceived conquest: you wanted to love him
and he you: Yours is the story too often repeated:
the city boy driven to alcohol, death:

But the willow once green is golden
and I remember you part in desire, part in fact:
You would have hated the lie I make of you; you
would have hated the fact:

Still the willow turns green to golden and still
you visit me in mid-morning, telling me of this awful
place, of the omnipresent *them*, who would not let you live
and I listen:

You who were too proud to equivocate: you who loved
    as freely
and deeply, as messily, as the world could imagine:
Paul, I miss you. I miss your hard-bearing, stern confidence,
your anger which made ghettos of all of us:

No one struggled more; no one asked more; no one
took the risk of presence more sacredly; in your loss
I understand not only the shores of grief,
but how its walls seem forever rising.

At first glance, Auburn Correctional Facility calls to mind a feudal castle or a stone and brick edifice worthy of Humphrey Bogart or Edward G. Robinson. One readily envisions prisoners dragging their balls and chains, the late-night prison break, or the lights slowly flickering, presaging the imminent electrocution. This is the stuff of movies, of prison lore. Yet for most of us, these images, dispatched out of Hollywood, are all we shall ever know about the real life in our nation's prisons. Most of us will certainly not be sentenced there; few of us will choose one as a place to visit.

Yet in every stereotype there is also a residuum of truth: people employ generalizations to celebrate a certain verity about the world; and no myth would have any currency if it did not, to some unassailable extent, identify something in actual experience. Certainly these cinematic incarnations are not the prison's reality, but they contain a grain of truth, nonetheless. Undeniably, though we may not know what a prison is, our imaginings, however incompletely, convey that the prison is a *hellish* place. Indeed, nothing in our arsenal of national fictions suggests that the prison is other than horrific. In this case, it is not a matter of correctness but of degree. The prisons—at least the prisons I have encountered—are infinitely more hellish than our Hollywood dream makers relate. Inmates in these places are not planning breakouts or prison riots; they are not planning anything. To dream of escape is to believe that one has something worthy of salvaging, to believe, that is, in the proposition of a self-orchestrated future. The prisons I have visited are spirit killers: the inmates—no matter how smart, capable, or engaging—have little sense of their own inextinguishable worth, their own human possibility. And this is not by accident.

Auburn Prison is certainly not the worst reformatory in this country, nor is it the best. Like most, it probably sits in the thick middle range: no inmate would ask to be sentenced there; certainly some might wish to be transferred out; a few of the hard-nosed might even like it, its attraction resting in its utter banality. Neither good (that is, experimental) nor bad (and the word here almost has no meaning, since Auburn, at least to my eyes—and no doubt to those of its inmates—is bad enough), Auburn just is.

At bottom, to cast out is not to cast off, and the long trek to Auburn Prison—through the mill town and over the proverbial railroad tracks—is our reminder that the great prison is a great industry: people earn their livings there; whole towns, including Auburn, are built on the day-to-day catering to our national pariah. And, like anything that both haunts and fascinates us, we come to the prison's gates armed with rocks and wonder.

Inescapably, and with great trepidation, we know that the inhabitants of our man-made Siberias are our brethren: indeed, it is this weighty realization, this sense that the murderer we so ruthlessly banish may not eternally quiet the potential murderer within, that so frightens us. For it takes but a few precious seconds for the mind's knife to become the hand's weapon. And all of us, at some terrible time, have walked that narrow footpath between the imagined and the horrific.

At Auburn, the first thing one confronts is its massive guard tower, with its rifle-shouldering, no-nonsense officer. By the time you have noticed him, he has noticed you. For a minute or so, he looks down at you, looks around you, and, always unsmiling, moves back to his elevation and privacy. What is so astonishing is that *you* feel condemned. You sense in that coldly dismissive gaze, in the backdrop of the great prison, that Gandhi was right: *to think of evil is to act evilly.* And you feel—and this is essential to the prison's apparatus—that the common denominator of your humanity had been discovered. That you are a writer, or a college professor, or a dutiful husband is of little significance. Here, as the guard corroborates, there is no room for romanticism: he's seen your kind before.

One enters Auburn Prison through two gigantic brass doors, each heavily tooled with elaborate metalwork, at the center of which, like an uneasy coupling, sits the famous symbol of Justice, with its blindfolded woman supporting her two delicately balanced weights. The rest of the portraiture is oddly cherubic, even sexual, as it seems the neoclassical invariably is. It is a celebration of everything, or a reminder of how everything— be it lust or justice—fights in this great amphitheater of a world. I wonder how I might understand this, should I be a prisoner passing on my way to serve a life sentence. He, certainly, knows that life is a great chaos—though this, I hazard, was not the artist's intention. It is, however, a possible interpretation; and it certainly was mine.

The prison's receiving room is reminiscent of an airport security check area, with much the same ingenious technology. At Auburn, there are two guards who inspect your clothing and carriables. Since I had come to read from my poetry, I had a canvas bag filled with books, and never have my works been so finely perused. Each page was rigorously examined; the bag was checked and rechecked.

After all of us had passed through the metal detector, the guard stamped our right hands with an invisible substance. Then we were counted. Indeed, at the next twelve checkpoints we were counted and counted again. At each checkpoint there is a "lock-in": a holding area where one must remain until a guard electronically dislodges the massive gates. The twelve of us, eleven teachers from Elmira Community College's Inmate Higher Education Program and myself, journeyed from check- point to checkpoint like wary salmon. The group was a strange conglomeration. All, with the exception of myself, were white; two of the twelve were women. Six had taught at Auburn for the last two years, and four had worked at the prison for more than a decade. One of the teachers, who wore a jaunty red hat, was the frailest young man I had ever seen. I wondered how he had negotiated his twenty-five years, not to mention the prison's exactings. Yet no one was particularly large or muscular. Sporting his Special Forces army jacket, one man nearly looked the part. But most were aging college and high school teachers, stomachs a notch wider, dreams a bit more remote, than all would like.

Finally we reached "the Yard" and began the long walk

through the corridor by Cellblock D. I say long walk, but it was only a thousand yards. All of a sudden, as if in a wall of sound, the prisoners began chanting "Baby, you're beautiful" to the two women with us. Loosened through the stone and Plexiglas, the sound recalled that haunting, terrifying Malabar Caves sojourn in Forster's *A Passage to India*, where human inadequacy and racism are shown as helpmeets. I kept thinking, *this is not sound, it is an indictment.* And then I realized, undeniably, shamefully, as if for the first time, what it must *cost* to be a woman, to have your body become, day in and day out, the receptacle for so much need, so much ill-digested, inchoate, dangerously poised lust.

I watched as the two women bore it, the college-aged one as strong as a serf in a Breton painting. Quickly her thin face closed down; she walked with a studied, disciplined bearing. Then someone, everyone yelling: *I'll kill you white motherfuckers.* The sound booming and pounding, as if the prison were a giant tuning fork.

Auburn Prison, built in 1816, is one of the oldest maximum security institutions in the United States. A pioneer in penology, Auburn was constructed with individual cells for each inmate, although the original design for these cells, the so-called Auburn System, was pernicious to say the least. During the early part of the nineteenth century, Auburn became the focus for a unique penal "experiment," in which the most incorrigible inmates were sentenced to absolute, uninterrupted solitary confinement. Permitted neither to leave their cells nor to read or work, the one hundred "selected" inmates were forced to stand for eight hours a day in total silence. Moreover, in the disturbingly convoluted thinking of the time, this practice was considered "a humane gesture," since it was assumed that an eternity of forced motionlessness might lead to muscle atrophy. No one, of course, questioned whether solitary confinement was itself inhumane. No, in the rigidly Calvinistic teaching of the day, a prisoner's lot was to be cruel. One burned in hell for one's sins; and prison, most certainly, was this earth's hell.

As might be surmised, in the first year of this heinous experiment, of the hundred prisoners involved, nearly half went mad, while the others succumbed to tuberculosis and pneumonia. Yet, as is so often the case with prisons, the public was of two minds: on the one hand, it wanted its "custodial houses" to keep the dangerous miscreants away from the community; it expected the prison to salve the commonwealth of a serious problem. On the other hand, it was only willing to permit the prison such "corrective leeway" as might preserve the community's conscience. Clearly, although the public had wanted these Auburn convicts to be severely punished, it did not wish to see them die in plaguelike numbers, at least not within *its* institution. And so, after its first barbarous year, the experiment was ended.

Yet ideas die slowly, and the Auburn penologists—zealots that they were—still believed that solitary confinement was the only way to discipline the abject criminal. Indeed, just two years after their first ill-fated attempt, they began a new, yet no less severe, improvisation on the same theme. Realizing that absolute, forced human isolation encouraged death and psychosis, the Auburn authorities proposed a modified system where inmates would work in a closely monitored common area, always returning to their individual cells to sleep. Although the prisoners might come in contact with one another at work and at meals, at no time would they be permitted to talk, exchange letters, or communicate. In 1822, this rigid denial of human intercourse—which is still the rubric in many of the world's penal systems—found its most eloquent spokesperson in Auburn's Warden Gersham Powers:

> The demands of nature must indeed be complied with; [the prisoners'] bodies must be fed and clothed ... but they ought to be deprived of every enjoyment arising from social or kindred feelings and affections; of all knowledge of each other, the world, and their connections with it. Force them to reflection, and let self-tormenting guilt harrow up the tortures of accusing conscience, keener than scorpion stings; until the intensity of their sufferings subdues their stubborn spirits, and humbles them to a realizing sense of the enormity of their crimes and their obligation to reform.

34

Fortunately, the Auburn Prison of 1822 is not the institution that one confronts today. In 1986, as a case in point, even the term *prison* is anachronistic: Auburn is a "correctional facility." Yet, even though Warden Powers is long buried, his philosophy, I surmise, still informs these halls. For Auburn, like any architecturally planned, functional structure, was constructed to facilitate a certain notion of reality. When these long tiers of individual cells were created—small, dark, and cramped—certain expectations were being fulfilled, certain others suggested. The prisoner in 1986 will not die from long hours of standing in his cell, as fifty of his brethren once did; but he still will find his room terribly constrictive; he still will notice how the walls of his cell jut out into the corridor, a further hindrance to "unwanted talk"; and he still will discover—and this he will relish, albeit silently—that this is *his* cell, however cramped, squalid, and dark.

This, of course, is no insignificant development. However small his quarters, the inmate possesses something which is *his*. He can hang something on the wall (provided he has something to hang) and can, as much as is humanly possible, leave his mark on his space. For a time, he does not have to worry about someone else's belongings, feelings, or privacy—at least while *they* are in *their* cells. And if you are a prisoner, this is essential and important rest. Certainly, one may murder oneself in one's own cell; but among the prison community, there are literally hundreds of people who might potentially murder you, and all for some supposed slight, and one not even necessarily directed at them but at their friend, lover, or even, God knows, at someone who is just a resident of their cellblock. In one's cell—for a few precious hours then—one can safely "watch one's back." Of course, there might be a fire, and one might perish; but there might be a nuclear disaster in New York, and all New York might evaporate in the conflagration. A prisoner, like most New Yorkers, is willing to live with that possibility. But he does not relish placing his life in harm's way, among people who know all too much about harm. And thus, his cell is, in this darkest of places, "heaven sent."

Yet none of this enlightened humanitarianism—which social architects might applaud and Anton Chekhov, weary of Sahalin, might understandably envy—has much effect on the visitor. He is far too much a victim of his own life, and the perilous nature of it. If he has not valued his freedom before coming to Auburn, if he has not thought about who he is (and therefore what he must protect), he does so now. For, whatever else a prison does, it demands that one confront it. If you are a prisoner, it might take you a dozen years to realize that the life you hope to create requires, above all else, that it be lived within these walls, for *these walls do not go away.* Here, of all the world's places, there is everything to accept.

For those of us who are *visiting*—and this, indeed, is the greatest privilege—our status is in our faces, our movements, our bowels. We know, and we cling to this as we might to our children, that *we shall walk out of here, tonight, at a certain hour.*

And it is just this privilege which both the prisoners and, to a lesser degree, the guards wish to cost us dear. When we walk through the corridors, the catcalls, the *Baby, you look beautiful* and *I'll kill you white motherfuckers,* were an expression of lust, anger, and bitterness; but they were also an expression of our enviable ability to put off that which the inmates could not elude. In our quick, stuttering movements, in our downturned faces, in our trying to look courageous, we possessed a vulnerability—and how powerfully, in a different way, we sensed it— that they could ill afford. Indeed, it was this flabby indulgence, this possibility for openly embracing fear (swimming in it, as one might a fur coat), for which they despised us. Fear would set them to the barbells late at night; fear would turn them taciturn; fear would cause them to stuff the fork into another's ribs before he jabbed it into theirs. Fear was *not* that mad dash between buildings, that shrinking, scared, trying-to-look-not-so movement which so claimed us.

36

I had been invited to Auburn Correctional Facility to read and talk about my poetry for an incredible two-and-a-half-hour class. I remember how my stomach tightened when I first learned that I had to perform for that length of time. By nature I am a one-hour person. Indeed, whenever I attend a lecture that swells on beyond that point, I find myself imaginatively melding with the audience, thinking how I must meet someone in three minutes, catch the late bus, or do the laundry. But more accurately, I clung to the question of time because it was the easiest thing on which to cling. Although it would be difficult to fill one hundred and fifty minutes, my great confrontation was not with the clock but with those time would place before me.

The forty inmates who made up my class were participants in Elmira Community College's Inmate Higher Education Program. Most of the students were black and in their early twenties; one man had gray hair. Conspicuously, the three white prisoners clustered together, in much the same way blacks often huddle together in the outer world. At Cornell, where I teach, this behavior is often looked upon as unfriendly at best and racist at worst. Few whites would concede that blacks, like themselves, are merely desirous of fraternizing with people with whom they share a common interest and experience. Whites, because this is America, have never had to justify their actions; they sit with and entertain whomever they wish. Yet when blacks exercise the same human prerogative, it is considered an act of dismissal, subterfuge, or war.

At Auburn I couldn't help but wonder what those white inmates felt with the tables turned. Was their isolation that of the lonely island or the citadel beyond assault? Clearly they were in the minority in the prison population, but they were also white; and I sensed, even in this last outcrop of civilization, that their color still had some sting. And even if it didn't call the heavens down, it did testify that they were, in prison parlance, some "bad muthafuckas." The few whites who found themselves sent up to Auburn had been convicted of repeated, unusually brutal offenses. Indeed, the viciousness of the whites' crimes seemed in inverse proportion to their numbers. As one of the black inmates described them, and not without a touch of envy, "if evil walked, them cats be Jesse Owens."

At Auburn one thing was immediately apparent: the inmates were delighted that I had come. In the first instance, I was someone they didn't know, who took them away from the tedium of the ordinary; but, more importantly, I was the first black teacher they had encountered in twelve months. Once I read two poems, the questions began: Where had I been raised? What was my background? How had I managed to evade prison? I breathlessly explained that I had grown up in Harlem, among two good parents "who rode my ass," but I offered little else.

This, of course, was an oversimplification, if not a direct lie. I had been raised in Harlem, but in the most unusual of circumstances. My father was a physician, my mother was a brilliant artist and writer, and I had attended one of the finest— and personally, most ruinous—independent schools in the city. I lived in Harlem, which is to say that I saw much, but I certainly hadn't lived the lives these inmates had. Indeed, I had spent my entire life keeping myself at a safe remove from anything that might bring me to Harlem's reality. Yes, I had done a little of this and a bit of that, but I was always at the sidelines. I knew where the deep water was—everyone knew that. But I remained a shore bird.

My brother, however, paid for my escape. A talented drummer, who shared the same IQ as myself (something my mother was always wont to remind me), he lived in those streets, and it, and the difficult contradictions he faced, broke him. My brother, Paul, would ultimately drink himself to death at age twenty-nine. He was tough, independent, and full of bitterness. He was, as I read that evening, "hungry for the end of the world."

The inmates particularly liked my "brother" poems. They too had brothers they missed and loved, brothers whose ultimate lives might be even more menaced than their own. This I found oddly comforting. In our desire to transcend the horror of crime, we hasten to view the criminal as someone without any notion of family or community. Certainly, this is our clumsy way of insulating ourselves from *their* human truth: for it is far too frightening to imagine ourselves as potential criminals, and far more convenient, and comforting to see the criminal as truly subhuman. Indeed, had they been born with twelve heads or twenty spikes, we might finally, irrevocably, be able to divorce ourselves from them. But as they come with two arms, two legs, a pumping heart, and a wondrous mind, their profanation suggests our own ratty flesh; their banishment, our own ever possible exile.

In truth, the lies we fabricate to distance ourselves from others invariably rise to haunt us. We may lie *to* ourselves, but others are under no obligation to lie *for* us. Whatever these inmates were—and all of them were sentenced to Auburn for corporal crimes—they would not permit me to view them merely as maniacs, psychopaths, or what have you. They were people, cussed and joy-filled, people capable of tenderness and murder, people like me, and yet unlike me, because I haven't yet, thank goodness, killed anyone.

I learned a great deal in those two hours and thirty minutes; much more, I trust, than those inmates learned from me. At one point, one of the students asked me to describe how it felt to enter the prison. I shall never forget how dangerous that question seemed to me, dangerous because it gave voice to all my inner disquiet. Quickly, I found myself looking about the room, noticing that there were no guards within immediate reach. To this day I don't know what made me sense my immediate vulnerability. Certainly it had to do with the poignancy of the question, for in some profound way, the inmate was asking me to unburden myself, to tell him how I had found a means to live with fear; yet just as centrally—and this was as palpable as air— he wanted to know if I thought he was a beast, if I had cast him beyond the shores of humanity (and if I had, he might make my suspicions *real*); but most fundamentally, most crucially, I realized that he, Lord knows how, had given language to my own questioning, my own inadequate "sew work." I hadn't made peace with the prison, with him, or with myself. And he knew it.

After some time—it seemed like hours; it was merely seconds—I told him the truth. I stated that the prison was the most frightening, scary place I had ever seen. He was quiet for a moment, and then he smiled. He agreed with me. *Agreed with me.* Yes, this place was as hellish as he imagined. In my own terror, I had thought that he had been holding me to my life; in truth, I had been holding him to his. He, like all of us, needed to affirm that his own powers of discrimination were accurate, that his experience might be mirrored by others. Although Auburn was brutal and spirit crushing, it had not yet destroyed his ability to perceive and differentiate shades of horror; it had not yet destroyed him. To this, at least, I could bear witness.

There were two questions that were asked again and again of me. Inmate after inmate wanted to know if I thought I would continue to write and to teach. At first, I was not at all surprised at this question: it is a common one, asked eternally of writers. Yet on this particular occasion, whenever I attempted to answer the question, the audience would neither hear nor accept my response. Again and again I would state that yes, I thought I would continue to teach, and again and again I would be presented with the same question. It was maddening.

Finally I realized what was happening. To these inmates, my tacit belief in the probability of an *assured* future, my notion that I could reasonably expect to find myself in a *certain* circumstance, at a *certain* time, was as mind-boggling as if I had just sprouted wings. For them, there had never been *one* veritable day of certainty. When they were in the streets, they had to live on mother wit; now, in prison, every minute brought new perils. Indeed, if there was one inexpugnable axiom for them, it was the present tense, the resounding *I am.* Of nothing else could they be certain.

Ultimately, their questions were, if you will, *pre-*questions: they were the first tentative vocalization of wonder. The inmates wanted me to repeat myself, because they could not understand the specifics of my answer, until they understood the astonishing grammar from which it sprang. Miraculously, although we shared the ability to make sounds, we had yet to forge a common language. And it was just this that made us tongue-tied at revelation: having so much to say, and no means, no suitable lexicon for conveying it, we were exiles in a country more hideous, terrible, and unreachable than any Kafka had ever imagined.

If Auburn cut the prisoners off from the world, it, more horribly, sealed them into their *futureless* selves. Usually, thankfully, human beings—because of imagination, spirit, and plain cantankerousness—evolve the means to transcend most anything, even the grim ghetto of self. Yet at Auburn, and I trust at most prisons, this could not be tolerated (*jails, we must remember, are to keep people in*). As any jailer knows, the walls of the present are always dismantled in the future; but if there is *no* future, if there is no ability to set aside and reconstitute, to interdict and reposition, then the present becomes the almighty, and the walls become unconquerable. Although I did not interview the jailers, I did see the jailed. For most of them, the walls without had become the walls within; and such walls never, no matter what Joshua does, *come a-tumbling down*.

After I had finished reading, one student, who had heretofore been silent, spoke up, reminding me that although "we prisoners might seem like nice guys, we're here because we killed people," the last statement clearly intended to elicit a reaction from me, the naive college professor. Now, after two long hours, I found myself getting angry. I wondered why he so wanted to frighten me, especially since it seemed that my easy fright was all he desired. But then I realized that he might be attempting something far more humanly essential and generous. As I had told him of my brother, had offered that intimate bond of personal experience and blood, so too would he share his only sacred gift—his experience—with me. Difficult and tentative as his motions were (and confession, by nature, is always stony), this man wanted to speak to me man to man, witness to witness.

What first I had taken as a vitriolic assault was merely this man's life: he had offered it up, in the ready language at his disposal. I might not like the life he had, or the brutal language by which he expressed it, but I certainly should permit him his truth. It might sting; I might refuse to listen; but this is the privilege of the listener. The teller, sadly, can only recount his tale: he can lie, but that, in itself, is just another corner of revelation.

At bottom, this man was trying to claim his humanity, as he tested mine. If I had my naïveté to lose, he had something far more essential to win—his personhood—and he would struggle for that at all costs. Indeed, it was the lopsidedness of this battle, the vast inequality of our two involvements, that so charged the moment. I, since I had not yet truly become pariah, had the privilege of arguing over the nature of my privilege (or even tossing it away if I so desired); while he, on the other hand, had no choice but to plead for his essential humanity. He, certainly, would not choose to walk into this prison—not with what he knew. Indeed, if there was light at the end of the proverbial tunnel for him, he had to create not only the light but the instrument by which it might be seen. And since our predicaments were far from being reciprocal, the wolves loomed at every corner.

And yet, remembering my childhood joy when I "acted the nigger" on the New York City bus, negotiating that delicious netherworld that only the marginalized are allowed, I understood what that inmate felt. When those "high-class" whites saw me, the chocolate-faced boy, they knew that I was the flesh-and-blood repository of their assumptions—the authentic ghetto type; and I, even though I attended the crème-de-la-crème private school in the city, gave them a show worthy of their concern. Although I didn't have any real power, I could certainly fool those people. I'd talk jive, look evil, and "bad-mouth" the toughest-looking white boy I could find. And then, laughing all the way, I'd romp over to the Collegiate School, the place where ninety percent of *their* children failed to gain entrance.

Yet, notwithstanding my minor triumph, I bitterly decried the subterra in which it was purchased. Certainly one can, in extreme cases, extricate some pleasure out of hell; but hell is nonetheless hell; it is certainly never heaven. And thus the inmate, though he needed me to facilitate his journey to self-announcement, could excuse neither the brashness of my declaration—I was asking him to justify himself—nor the insubstantiality of my presence. Whatever else I was, to him, and the rest of the prison population, my credentials were dubious at best. A Cornell professorship might mean something in the outer world, but here, it was as valuable as an expired driver's license or an old football ticket. Power, we must remember, is only negotiable where it has validity. In the prison, had I been physically strong or good at cards, I might expect a measure of admiration, respect, and fellowship; but *sans* these talents, my degrees and professional standing, understandably, met with little interest. Indeed, the value system that had so honored me had exiled them. For those who had been ritually cast out, certainly, it would be an inhumanly bitter pill to swallow to be expected to salute the son as they suffered under his father. Blake to the contrary, the cut worm does *not* forgive the plow.

Ultimately the human voice is a very wondrous thing: it can show, at rare moments, everything that propels it. That these men had once been murderers meant that they could also be something else; at least, that was what the new wavering in this young man's voice suggested. I watched him slowly negotiate the incline of possibility, his voice swelling into a trill of astonishment, at first slow, gravelly, and then steady. Certainly this wasn't a wave of spontaneous announcement; he had seen far too much for that. More, it was the hard, pruned, strained depth taking of someone who sensed, albeit bitterly, that the world might return nothing. But still he, with no reason that I could fathom, kept speaking, his own narrative building, gathering. Suddenly, words suggested words, listening suggested listeners, confession suggested healing; and he said, both to himself and to me, "Man, you ain't bad." And that was enough.

43

At ten o'clock, the bell rang, and the prisoners began to file back to their cells. Of the forty I spoke with, twenty or so came up to me, shook my hand, and asked if I might come back. None of these congratulations came from the three white prisoners, something I can only presume to understand. My poems are not overly racial; I didn't read a large number of racial poems. Possibly I had neglected them; possibly they did not like my reading. I just do not know.

The journey out of the prison seemed more efficacious. When we entered the yard this time, it was filled with inmates pumping iron, smoking, and chatting. Again we were escorted by four guards. Now the towers, with their no-nonsense sentries, were well lighted, although the lights were not dancing over the grounds as in the movies. For the first time I looked at the one-hundred-year-old granite. These walls had been made to last: Hell, as Gersham Powers had so wanted, would remain interminable.

Near the first checkpoint, I saw one of the inmates who had been at my seminar. He smiled—a long, good smile—a smile that seemed almost hungry, a smile much like my brother's. I wished him well.

Then we began the elaborate countings until we reached the last checkpoint, where they asked us to put our right hands under an ultraviolet light. The light illuminated the invisible stamp that had been placed on our wrists when we first entered the prison. It seemed such a fitting way to leave this place: the once invisible stamp, now glowing luminously green, as yet again another mystery.

The School

No one, after all, can be liked whose human weight
and complexity cannot be, or has not been,
admitted.

—James Baldwin

Improve the flying moments, the motto on the ancient
dead clock read, and every Collegiate boy, whether he was
rushing to homeroom, algebra, or the bathroom, would pass this
aphorism ten times a day and a million times a year. It is difficult
to tell what exactly its impact was on the three hundred or so
boys; it certainly did not have the force of New York City,
baseball, or the occasional glimpse of a lost girl who had somehow
found her way into the dark reaches of the school. It also
certainly never really found its mark, for we always noticed it on
the run, improving our lives possibly, but more hopelessly
concerned with our difficult bodies, which seemed forever to
have new designs on us. Though the school was founded on that
dream of purity, which I gather must be at the soul of one-sexed
schools, the lack of suitable context for one's overwhelming
bodily urges haunted everything. One can lie about the body, but
the body does not lie about itself. And so much of what happened
in those halls, to me and to others, happened, I believe, because
the school from its outset began casting out and cementing in.
The school would have no women, as it would have few blacks
and Jews; and the few elect who would enter its doors would be
a frustrated bunch indeed. Frustration is painful enough as it is:

45

frustration without any possibility for human redress—frustration, that is, which is institutionalized—sours and corrodes.

The Collegiate School, the oldest private school in America, was founded in 1638 when New York was New Amsterdam. The school underwent thirteen moves in location, each a response to some veracity of history—a fire, a war—and a student sensed that he was part of a large motion, a sweep that took in nearly everything. Even the great city, Whitman's "Manhatta," had learned to wait at the portals of the mighty school. Like fire, Collegiate had endured, and would endure; a student was certain of that. And a student, almost subconsciously, began the slow process of self-abnegation as he entered its walls, for like any grand notion, Collegiate demanded a constant ritual of reverence. Yes, it was true that you were a boy, and a good boy. But it was the school that was *great,* it was the school that had *elected* you; it was the school that had lasted for three hundred years, educating presidents and poets alike.

This truth was echoed in a million ways, should one ever have the temerity to doubt it. Your parents—if they were white—certainly reiterated the school's bloodline: the school, in a word, was the doorkeeper to life's opportunities, the first gauntlet. However, if you were one of the few black students, as I was, your parents were thrown into a sizable quandary. Although they understood what an education promised, they also realized, just as dramatically, that they were sending their children into enemy country, one that neither they nor their children had previously experienced. In the black community, as in all communities, one only places one's child in peril when the dangers are vastly outpaced by the opportunity for human fulfillment. In this case, the black parents could only act in the abstract: they could only do as their ancestors have so often done, and hope that the strength of their issue could meet the day's vicissitudes. Like their predecessors, they had to trust in the intrinsic value of the sojourn; they had to believe—and at such a mighty cost—that their children would meet with a better fate than they themselves had. In truth, for many of these parents, a shot in the dark was better than no shot at all. As Billy Preston sings, "nothing from nothing is nothing." And these parents had seen the ravages of the ghetto—they knew what the bleak streets of Harlem and Bed-Sty promised, knew the drugs, the ruination, the children turned to premature old men. It was understandable why these parents turned to the unknown, for at least the possibility for hope was not yet foreclosed. The ghetto world, they knew, promised little if not more of the same—and no one wanted to see more of the dead, the walking dead, the pimps, the junkies, the thousand ways in which the imagination is driven underground. And so these parents, however uneasily, offered their children to the white world.

I can't imagine how I was accepted into the Collegiate School, and it certainly was a mixed blessing. During the interview my parents tell me that I miraculously extended my hand to the then headmaster, Wilson Parkhill—a tall, lean, handsome man—and said, with the great gallantry that only the young can muster, "Bonjour." Now, since I didn't know any French then, I can't imagine what got into me; but whatever it was, it commenced a relationship with the school for the next twelve years. In fact, my small motion toward internationalism permitted me to enter a select body of twenty first-graders, the second black youngster to attend the Collegiate School in 318 years. Edward Boyd, the first, had entered in pre-primary just the year before. There we were, the *Two*, to struggle upstream for twelve more years. And what a struggle it was.

Even now it is difficult for me to write about the school, since much of my life seems so preoccupied with it. In truth, it is as if we are Siamese twins, sharing the same organs, while, at every possibility, trying to assert our individual identities. And this undoubtedly was what Collegiate wanted: it wanted to be part of your bloodstream. And it was certainly this design on my person, Lord knows, which I adamantly resented and resisted.

Still, twelve years is a long time, and the wages of struggle, like the scars, are undeniable. I haven't, like many of my classmates, proudly become a Collegiate boy—I am, thank goodness, not yet a masochist. But I must admit that as much as these scars fester and sting, they are also largely what I am. I may despise my history, but it is still my history. Although a one-legged man may hate his missing limb, he doesn't cut off his good leg. No matter what his handicap, he has found an equilibrium, something that is sacred. And so let me just state that I went for twelve years to a place—twelve seminal years—and whatever the passage, I paid its price. There are many things that I am and many things I am not. I am a bundle of confusions, ambivalences; I am also, at times, happy, awed, ecstatic. Collegiate permitted me, I must admit, the language to enter my despair; one day it will also permit me, I surely hope, the language to rid myself of it.

In some very real way, I can't tell whether I hate the school for providing me with the diagnosis or with the possible cure; the pain, in both cases, is real, immense.

Collegiate for me, and I think for Ed Boyd, though possibly not as dramatically, was pure hell. He lived on the West Side near Columbia, in one of the most dynamic and wonderfully integrated communities in the world. With the university, Riverside Church, Union Theological Seminary, and a host of other institutions, Ed was surrounded by mankind's testimonials to fellowship. I, on the other hand, though living on a very pretty, quiet street in Harlem, lived in Harlem, which is, however else one might wish to describe it, a ghetto. And a ghetto, all pyrotechnics deleted, is nothing more than a group of people who share a common identity. My sojourn from home to Collegiate, from one ghetto to another, was a startling and frightening journey from one reality to another. Both of them were exacting—at home I had to live in a certain way, pay attention to various street rules, one of them being that I had best never forget that the street was not Collegiate in blackface; and at Collegiate, I had better never forget that I was not at home.

Indeed, two of my most startling remembrances concern just this loss of footing. Once while I was home, I made the mistake of forgetting my "place" while playing first base in a baseball game. In one of those close plays at the bag, I recall arguing with a kid who adamantly felt that he was "safe." We debated, gesticulated, stomped around; and then I remember stating, after he offered something irrefutable, that he "had a valid point." In a second, he was in my face, grabbing my collar, ready to punch my words back. "What was that?" he asked. And, though only in the third grade, I realized what I had done. I had used a word that he didn't know—and a word that one didn't know, at least in my community, always signified derision.

But the ways of Collegiate were just as formidable, and any breach of decorum as sternly rebuked. When my parents sent me off to Collegiate they provided me with one weapon for the many they wished they could supply. It was the admonition to suffer no racial insult, to use my fists if such an offense occurred. Upon my arrival at Collegiate, it was painfully obvious that I was different (and I am not only speaking about my lack of a Rolls Royce or a New England accent). The boys, in truth, didn't fully understand the parameters of my difference—they only felt, no doubt, the sense of my intrusion, my dis-ease. And I presume this notion that I was so bothered by them necessitated the nagging premise on their part that they were somehow responsible for my discomfort, something that further suggested to them that *they*, Lord knows how, were responsible for *me*. Now, for children—and that is what we were—this is quite a mouthful to swallow; and since children, like their elders, have wonderful defense mechanisms, it is not difficult to understand why racial epithets became—at least for some—an easy rubric for dis-placement. So, on a warm spring day, John Ewing made the mistake of calling me *nigger*. And I, not suffering this for an instant, socked him.

Well, Collegiate was not ready for this, and two days later my mother was called in to speak with the assistant principal. For a few moments, as my mother tells it, they exchanged pleasantries, even announcing their shared interest in gardening (my mother has always loved plants and can grow nearly anything, even in the city). After a time, understandably, my mother asked why she had been so summoned, and the story of my behavior—*Kenny is usually such a wonderful, responsible boy*—was laid out for my mother's scrutiny. The principal, to her credit, completely deplored John Ewing's action; she and the school, as my mother must understand, would never condone such sentiments. But I had not responded as a Collegiate boy should. Yet, before the assistant principal could explain what I in fact had done, my mother, upon hearing the word *nigger*, broke in, asking her if I had hit the boy. The assistant principal said yes, expecting the appropriate denigration of my action, when my mother, her face as openly prideful as she might have been when discussing her prized gladiolas, just stated, "Good for him." The assistant principal, of course, was speechless; she had not anticipated this. But more centrally, she was bowel-tied, for she had, like all liberals, innocently believed that the new family was the same as her own, whatever their coloring—the lively discussion of flowers had just reaffirmed this notion. When we entered Collegiate, we, like everyone else, would fast become members of the Collegiate family— the rules, like the ability to walk, would just assert themselves. But in that little office the assistant principal was confronting the notion that she had no *notion* of us—that we, though we had entered the school and loved flowers, were an unknown quantity. This is where most social interactions end: the problem looking so large, so incomprehensible. But it is also the crucial center for possibility, for the facts, though difficult, are finally apparent. No matter what, one must realize that the black world and the white world are indeed worlds with elaborate rituals and customs. As it has taken three hundred years to become an American white, so too has it taken three hundred years to become an American black. Indeed, it is as dangerous to underestimate the gulf between the two American cultures as it is injurious not to attempt to bridge them. As in a Chekhov story, the facts not taken into account—such as human cussedness— are still the facts. Although one can fashion a boat out of cement, sink it will.

The assistant principal, that day, though she barely knew it, was confronting the void, the great chasm between black and white people. She, understandably, as a white had believed that her premise would hold true for black people— people, naturally, generalize from their own experience, and thus the horror we see again and again in international diplomacy. In effect, the assistant principal had assumed that the lives of black people had remained stationary while the lives of her own people had progressed. Although my family and I had historically been denied entrance into the school, she reasoned that we, once admitted, would welcome our new benefactors with no sense of the lateness of the day or the incomprehensible nature of our previous denial. Oh, if it were only true that "the cut worm forgives the plow." But it is probably more judicious to ac-knowledge that the person one has slighted will remain forever at the gates of revenge. It is easy to forget the day one stole one's brother's shoe, but the blisters on his feet are etched indelibly in his memory.

Clearly much of the assistant principal's sentiment comes, I think, from one's need for self-protection, for to under-stand the anger and betrayal that blacks must feel would be tantamount to understanding one's act of complicity. No one wants to accuse oneself of crimes against the human spirit—and few, indeed, do. But these questions notwithstanding, black people, like humanity everywhere when confronted with a difficult reality, fashioned lives: they had children, honed plans, found jobs when they could, suffered, and laughed. Most impor-tantly, they walked in the world with a history, an appreciation of those elements that had sustained and endangered them. White people might not acknowledge these things, but they were true nonetheless. And thus, when my mother and the assistant principal began their conversation, three hundred years (and indeed centuries of lives in Europe and Africa) hung over the room like a sword.

Not all of my problems with Collegiate had to do with race; indeed, many of them, I suppose, related to my general personality, though for a black person one's personality and what people make of one's life are often difficult to untangle. The prevailing educational philosophy of Collegiate was: always make the student feel inadequate. Thus, you could be in the first quadrant of your class and have an 80 average; students would routinely fail; in my twelve years at Collegiate, I would hazard that fifteen percent of the student population was asked to leave. And I must admit that Collegiate was brutally equitable in these exactings: it would throw out the sons of financiers, publishers, educators—the most distinguished names in America. On one point Collegiate was eminently fair: it was hell for everyone. And the results were just as awesome: when I was in the fifth grade, of my class of thirty-four, eighty-five percent were seeing analysts. And this was more than mere fashion. In a school where the ages seemed to look down upon you, where your parents had invested a fortune, where the whole world, they said, wished to be, you didn't, in Snodgrass's rhetoric, "wear your Godhead lightly."

At Collegiate, students learned to take and accept grades of minus 40. In my math class, I recall that the teacher, after giving me a 28 on a quiz (60 was passing), invited me to show it to my English teacher and "beg for help." Such cruelty was daily fare. On another occasion, this same teacher, who because I wouldn't sleep with him or take low, decided to make an example of me. During lunch, each teacher was assigned a table to proctor and the math teacher had mine. Like all of the teachers, he imposed various rules, most of which were eminently understandable and logical—rules any courteous person was delighted to respect. But on the day in question, I had begun eating my dessert without finishing my food, a cardinal sin. I remember him chiding me, "Kenny, we don't begin eating our dessert without finishing our food," with that high nasal whine that still induces nausea in me. For my part I was not being disrespectful; I was just hungry. The food that day was particularly inedible—I was, teacher or no, going to eat something. And as I asked to be excused, I remember the smirk on the teacher's

52

face. I would have hell to pay, and the next class, in some fifteen minutes, would be his.

As soon as the bell sounded, the math teacher called on me, wanting the answer to number 44. The textbook, as was the rule those days, numbered the problems at the level of their difficulty: number 1 was easiest and number 44 was the most demanding (indeed, I knew of no one who could regularly do the most difficult problem). Before I could get my textbook open, the teacher was already shrilly asking, "Kenny, did you do your homework?" Then, before I had the opportunity to explain that I had indeed done my homework—at Collegiate, one would always do one's homework, in fear of public ridicule— the teacher motioned me up to the board and commanded me to proceed through the problem. At first, understandably, I was hesitant. I hadn't been able to solve it at home when I had unlimited time; now, with no leisure, I had to do the impossible. But I made a few stabs, tentative as they were. With each chalk fall, the teacher became more livid, asking the class, over and over, "Isn't that stupid?" Finally, after a few moments, I just quit, collecting myself. Then I uttered what I knew was going to call the heavens down: "I know you want me to say I am stupid, but the only stupid person here is you." And I was sent to the headmaster.

The next morning I told my parents that I was not going to Collegiate anymore, that I couldn't tolerate it. Thinking about their response, I feel that my words just corroborated what they themselves thought but didn't wish to voice—that yes, God, we have sent our boy among wolves. For my parents, this was probably the most difficult situation they had ever encountered: my participation in the far-off world was premised on the most fragile of moorings, and now their boy was stating that he had come smack up against reality, and it was dark indeed. In many ways, my parents, like me, were adrift in something out of our ken—if the first step into the unknown had been my entrance into the school, we had long ago made peace with the universe, which was largely made up of our imaginings. Now, unfortunately, we had concrete information, and the universe was filled with death knells. Before, we could counter every fear with the fears—the substantiated fears—that surrounded us, for Harlem was nothing if it was not animated with the frightening. But now the world of the school was one full of trapdoors, and one wondered if one were just exchanging one hell for another.

Somehow I decided to return to school—I certainly don't know what made me. Knowing my father, he probably wove another layer of dreams, substantial enough to permit me to reenter the fray.

No doubt some of my difficulty with the school was exacerbated by my inclination to be artistic. Although Collegiate offered no creative writing electives, I soon found myself composing highly imaginative and flowery essays, the proverbial young writer with an undiminishable love for language. These efforts, of course, were hardly memorable; but in a world where I had so little of my own possession, these imaginative flights were crucial to me. As I was to appreciate later on, with the horror of my brother's death, my discovery of some true interest, some passionate identification, was life itself.

I remember how I would read my papers out loud at home, trying to get the prose to sound lyrical. I would write and rewrite, thinking of Frederick Douglass and Francis Bacon (the former part of my parents' required reading; the latter, the school's). Coming as I did from parents who told wonderful, full-bodied stories, and from a father whose narrative prowess rivaled Faulkner's, I held language in highest esteem. In my home, conversation was the greatest delicacy; one fell or triumphed by the virtuosity of one's oratory. With great relish my brother and I would squabble for attention, spinning the grandest yarns or telling the best jokes. Paul, who also attended Collegiate, was clearly the most adept. He would skillfully meld street language with school language, traversing the two dictions as if he were Lionel Hampton. I'll never forget one of his best lines, and this at age ten. Hearing of someone's death, Paul said, "Well, the dude got a pink slip from God."

54

On one of my more lyrical, free-wheeling papers, one Collegiate teacher wrote, "This shows too much imagination." Yet I shall never forget what took place when I submitted an optional paper on Ralph Ellison's novel *Invisible Man*. The teacher, Henry Adams, who, for all his shortcomings, was probably the finest interpreter of texts I have ever known, returned the paper with the underlined comment, "You must forget you are black when you write." I remember scribbling furiously in the margin of that effort, "You must forget you are white when you read it." But I didn't have the temerity to make my feelings known. In fact, much of my lingering sense of self-disappointment involves my inability at that time to express my rage. Like the protagonist in Ellison's novel, at every turn I was swallowing blood.

Interestingly, Mr. Adams would later do something in my senior year that I will never forget. Although I had done miserably in English with him, at times barely passing, one morning he called me to his desk and presented me with a catalogue to Dartmouth, his alma mater, suggesting I might consider it for the next year. I've never figured this out. He certainly didn't offer this to any of the other boys, many of whom had done far better than me. But I shall always remember that act of kindness and trust. My father would later tell him that I was doing A work in English at Cornell, and he would, in my father's words, just "smile benignly and wave his hand."

As the oldest independent school in America, Collegiate was a well-defined community, with strong assumptions and ideals. Coming largely from the same privileged backgrounds, its students had been in the process of nurturing this sense of community all their lives: if they had a world, it was certainly the school's. However, for the few black students—and the even fewer latino ones—this was not the case. I remember the brackish times when the two worlds came into obvious conflict. Unlike the other "prestige" schools, Collegiate was located on the West Side, in a neighborhood that was in some ever-horrific state of transition. Indeed, one had only to walk two feet from the school's elaborate Dutch Reformed architecture to buy nearly anything, be it drugs or women. The students, with the exception of a few Holden Caulfields, were rarely knowledgeable about any of this, since the "life" respected the institution or, more truthfully, the power of those who frequented it. The prostitutes and the pushers might not have had the school's education, but they knew a great deal about power. And the students—those cuddly, naive, flabby children—were the powerful. For as the street people knew, it took money to insure naïveté: they had only to recall how quickly their own children's eyes had wandered from childhood.

The West Side location of the school necessitated that many of its students take public transportation. I recall how one fourth-grader had waltzed out of the 79th Street crosstown bus, openly clutching a fifty-dollar bill in his hand. Now, I don't know why a ten-year-old boy had fifty dollars, nor can I understand why he was so obviously tempting fate; but when he came crying into the headmaster's office, explaining how he had been robbed by two teenagers, the school was thrown into a tizzy. The administration, the students, and the parents were all appalled. How could this happen? The other black students and I, though not insensitive to the students' fear—we had certainly lived long enough with those same fears ourselves—were incredulous in other ways. Our thinking: why would a boy be so stupid as to carry fifty dollars in his hands in the middle of the city? Here, as in the situation involving my mother and the assistant principal, was the central paradox: the school believed only in that narrowly defined notion of the city which was Park Avenue and safety, the place from which its students came and to which they would hopefully return, and wanted to run from any sense of the city as the brutal place it could be. We, who had always seen the city as brutal, who had honed our teeth on its cutting edge, could not be expected to share their surprise that two young hoods had lifted a rich boy's fifty-dollar allowance. We, on some level, envied those boys' pluck—it would be a long time till fifty bucks came our way. Moreover, the school's desire to flee the nagging reminder of the dark side of city life was, in truth, a desire also to flee us, since our lives were largely premised on the scourges of that reality. And, as you can well understand, it is a difficult predicament to find oneself among people who, at every turn, wish to deny your existence.

It was also true that we took a certain pleasure in knowing that "the rich white boys" would continue to get robbed. Certainly, the reality that had robbed them had also robbed us, but we weren't being philosophical. To us, our lives had been constantly menaced—and it was good to know that someone else had finally felt some pain. To a large degree these kids represented our trouble: they had money and we did not; they felt comfortable and we did not; they could get astonished at the brutality of New York as we could not. Indeed, it was this sense of privilege that we hoped would cost them dearly. At no point, not in Harlem and not at the school, had we ever felt comfortable. Discomfort rarely makes one generous; discomfort that seems forever one's lot, that seems never to be shared by others, makes one brutal. And so we—powerless in the real questions of fate—were ready with rocks at the public stoning grounds. And, as human history again and again asserts, the powerless are powerful in only one thing: hate for the powerful.

There was another important realm in which the black students and the white students parted company. As Collegiate was an all-male school, much of the dating revolved around the other independent schools, such as Brearly, Nightingale-Bamford, and Spence. These schools were, at least in my time, even less integrated than Collegiate, so should a black student even attempt to follow the social ritual, he would meet with much difficulty. In truth—and, considering the reality, most fortunately—most of the black students ceased their relationship with the school as soon as their academic day ended; they certainly didn't depend on it for their social activities. They, like me, lived a bifurcated existence: the two worlds kept as separate as one keeps a cobra from a mongoose. In the worst days of Southern segregation, the Klan posters used to read, "Niggers must be out of town by sundown." Well, we were out of town—white town, that is—at the close of math club, track practice, debate club, or biology lab.

I do recall, on a rare occasion when I was on the East Side, seeing one of my classmates walking arm in arm with a young woman. She was very lovely, and I remember wondering how Frank had done so well, since no one at school liked him, and there were so few people whom no one liked. Anyway, I came abreast of Frank and said hello, only to find his face fall like coal in a shuttle. Frank looked at me, said nothing, and walked away. This was no case of mistaken identity: we were only two feet from each other. I will never forget the absolute denial in his face. It was the face of someone who was casting one out of the sanctuary.

On the lighter side, there was also the time I went to the seventh-grade dance at the Brearly School. Because boys, at that awkward age, are enormously shy, the Brearly parents divided the class into manageable groups, each group meeting at the home of one of the girls, where they would be dined as a precursor to the dance. This whole business was done by name, the Collegiate roster distributed evenly among the host parents. When I received a lovely gilded invitation, my parents reasoned that I should go, even though I had my doubts. I should recount that my parents wanted me to partake of everything the school offered. They believed that we, at least, should fulfill our part of the bargain. Let it never be said that the American promise of equality had been thwarted by us. So, with a thousand reservations, I had my suit pressed and brought my host a corsage. And, as is so often the case, the pending preparations, the running here and there, the endless fanfare, the shoes not the right color, the nervousness—all contributed to the oddly exciting pathos of which the young remain forever victim.

I remember how I felt as I entered the Fifth Avenue apartment, feeling that everyone was in for a surprise, and wondering how they would react, how I might react to their reaction. When I finally reached the door, however, no one seemed at all surprised at the coffee-colored boy with the new suit and the wet hands. Indeed, I still wonder if the school had prearranged this; but I must also admit that one of the most difficult things about being black is the continual legacy of being astonished. One certainly cannot afford to throw caution to the winds, and thus one always travels with one's armor on. But what often happens—as it did the night of the dance—is that one gets the nagging feeling that one is betting against oneself. My God, what a pleasant surprise to be taken as a human being!

Interestingly, the dinner was such a joy—and I had so much fun—that I, even to this day, can barely understand it. The anger that I feel at myself (the anger that I presume many black people feel) is often buttressed by such occasions: Oh, how much more wonderful it could have been had I not come in there wearing the wariness of color. And yet this consciousness is my life. When teaching Afro-American literature, I often make a point of stating that I wake up each morning realizing my difference: when I look at the mirror I see that I am black. Now, this is not an attempt at soliciting empathy; I certainly do not wish or want that. Lord knows, I am delighted to be who I am. But this sense of difference is the leavening—the essential calibration—by which I survive. The younger generation seems not at all to be caught in my eddies: they have, as they should, a different improvisation. Many of them see themselves as human beings first, as blacks second. I, on the other hand, see myself as a black human being—my color as the dipstick, the barometer by which I test and measure the world. If the younger blacks can gaily walk on Fifth Avenue and more fully engage America's endless promise, then it is wonderful; I am happy for them. But I shall never walk without the constant sense of the struggle my identity has caused in others and in myself. In this way, at least at the present moment, I may be in a time warp. Yes, I am delighted if the black young are fulfilled. I only hope that they are. But delight, in itself, cannot turn me from the self I constructed, the concrete I poured to face the world.

At thirty-four, it seems strange to complain that I cannot change; but what one wants to believe and what one believes, at least in terms of one's reality, are very different things. In many ways I honed myself into a mechanism that was able—with some exceptions—to confront the world. In this I did what we all do. In truth, my worldview did not permit me to enjoy the fullest participation at the Brearly dance; no worldview is perfect. Yet, like any approximation, any attempt at creating a philosophy that is more embracing than not, more capable of dealing with a large field of possibilities than not, my self— narrow as it was—was the best I could fashion. James Baldwin argues that the most an American black can achieve is "a truce with reality." And my truce held me together. Yes, I wished I had not prejudged the Brearly family; yes, I wished I could have completely enjoyed the festivities without the nagging invoice of race. But let's face it, like Ellison's protagonist, my thatched self did permit me, if not all the frequencies, the possibilities of the thick middle range. It also permitted me to outlast Collegiate.

It's been fifteen years since I last set foot in a Collegiate classroom, and one would think I might have mellowed. In the interim, I have found a good job, a wonderful wife, and a small but comfortable house in the country. People often tell me that the school—"your fine background"—is largely responsible for this success. And there is certainly some truth to this. Yet the greatest legacy of the school is that of self-hatred. For many, I guess, the idea that you need forever to be confronted with how little you know is a missive to learn more. But for someone like myself, who has enough insecurities inbred, whose color is the greatest badge of difference and unacceptability, the constant reminder of one's shallow footing, the inevitable suggestion that one's stupidity is an ever-present fact, the day-in, day-out an- nouncement of one's inadequacy, these had but one effect: to nearly paralyze me. Yes, even now I still worry about my real intelligence. I wonder if I deserve my teaching position, my Phi Beta Kappa key, my books of poems. Collegiate said I was bright but shy. But I never did well there. Indeed, after a particularly bad year, I believe it was fifth grade, my IQ was retested. They found that I was the brightest boy in the class—or so they told me. But the next week, my mother said they thought I was dyslexic—that because I couldn't spell. Invariably, the problem rested with me, the school forever saying, *cast out the offending part.*

Collegiate, like any total environment, instilled things on many levels, some of which—whether they were intended or not—grew nefarious because they were never intellectually confronted. Like air, or the *improve the flying moments* adage, they were imbibed by untold thousands of us without the slightest comment—their importance, interestingly, accentuated by the fact that in the most intellective of places, their significance was never questioned. Since the school was arguably the finest school in New York City—one had only to look at the thousands of applications for the twenty or so places in the first-grade class or at the college placements of its seniors—it was understood by inference that those not included among its body were somehow lacking. Notwithstanding the thousands who could not afford to come—or who could not, the numbers dictating, find a berth—the complete inadmission of women was the greatest curse. If Collegiate was where one found the finest minds, it was obvious that women, since they were not in attendance, were not of the elect. And so thousands of us had this ill-digested sentiment that women were only for our weekend play. More frighteningly, without women in our midst, we could conceive of them as creatures totally alien to us. Certainly, we knew that they were important—we had mothers—but we didn't know a thing about them. In such a state, we would often be so insecure, so stupid, so lust-ridden, that the weekend encounter would be either the worst experience imaginable (for the Brearly woman, quite rightly, did not see herself as the inelect) or, more horribly, a situation one inch removed from rape—and I speak here not only of the act, for the denial of a woman's mind, her ability to think, to be a person, was the logical outcome of men who knew women as only the fantasy shapes of their locker-room talk. I recall how everyone always spoke of scoring. *Well, what happened?* What could possibly happen when you were so uptight that you were not a real person to the woman, and she, certainly, was not a real person to you? The Collegiate boy was not really interested in scoring; he was interested in meeting the other half of humanity, that half which he intuited was important, essential, and desirable. He might not yet know why, but the human personality—Collegiate to the contrary—argued for wholeness, for men and women to see each other as persons, sacred in their difference but undeniable in their interdependence.

My brother spent twelve years at the school, and his experience was even more horrible than mine. By nature, Paul was more of a loner than I; he was also more truculent, more sensitive, in a more complex and remote way. From the fifth grade on, Paul had little to do with the school; he went to classes, but he lived for his return to Harlem. Indeed, in one of his English classes, the teacher, probably with some sense that Collegiate did in fact belong to New York City, asked his students to write on Claude Brown's article "Growing Up in Harlem." Paul, who lived there, wrote nothing; he just turned in a blank sheet of paper. My mother was incredulous at this; she couldn't understand why he just didn't write about what he knew. Paul never explained his inaction. But I recall that about the same time we visited George Washington's home in Arlington, Virginia. I, for my part, found myself quickly bored with the historical things and wanted to gaze out at the river, calculating how George might have tossed the dollar across its waters. However, my brother, upon encountering the slave quarters, spent the entire time looking at its artifacts. Paul never spoke about this experience, but it was obvious that it had strongly claimed him.

By the time Paul was to graduate, he had so sufficiently alienated himself from the school that even his imminent graduation was in question. The school, as you might expect, had a very rigorous sense of student decorum: your hair had to be a certain length, you had to wear a jacket and tie, and no one was permitted to wear facial hair. Paul had a huge Afro, and had been warned that if he were to graduate, much of it would have to be shorn. Well, Paul waited until the last moment to have it cut; it was finally trimmed at ten-thirty on the day of his graduation, with just enough time to show the results to the headmaster. Paul dallied not only as an act of rebellion but because he really didn't care what Collegiate wanted—the "white boys," he would call them. To him, the place was full of dead heads. It was full of those who ran Harlem, the enslavers. Paul finally relented when my father suggested that if he would get his hair cut, he could effectively distance himself from the school forever. This sounded good to Paul. And so he walked through the school's doors one last time.

My brother would later drink himself to death, in a tale too painful to recount here. I maintain that my brother's death was caused by a number of forces—race, the age, his inability to find something to be truly passionate about. Still, his schooling, like my own, did not provide him with the proper sustenance to transcend the world. Surely a school is not a parent, and a school cannot guarantee a person's life or happiness. But I believe a school can foster an environment where a student's sense of self is supported. For my brother and myself, Collegiate only interchanged one minefield for another: we knew we could die in Harlem; we would later learn that we could die at Collegiate.

Perhaps this is a valuable lesson: the world is vicious everywhere. But I presume that the courage that permitted us to enter the white halls of the Collegiate School was real courage—courage which, if mined and affirmed, might have made us strong, well-adjusted persons. This certainly isn't idle hope; it is the premise of every educational institution, Collegiate included. For many, Collegiate, I know, fulfilled its mission: ninety-five percent of my classmates see their excellent lives as direct result of the school's work. But I, more frightened now than I ever was when I first encountered its walls, wonder if I might have been better off going to the dreadful school in my neighborhood, with its bad teachers and ill-supported programs, encountering its vexations, its manifold dangers. This now, of course, is a moot question; but that it remains a question at all is horror enough.

Unity Day

Does man love Art? Man visits Art,
   but Art squirms.
Art Hurts. Art urges voyages—
and it is easier to stay at home,
the nice beer ready. . .
         —Gwendolyn Brooks,
           "The Chicago Picasso"

Perhaps these are not poetic
      times
      at all
         —Nikki Giovanni,
           "For Saundra"

I am fond of telling my creative writing students that in a time of true crisis one often finds oneself focused on something oddly trivial, something that becomes, God knows why, as important as the Rosetta Stone in one's present moment of distress. This "new obsession" can be as banal as the color of one's toothbrush or the realization, albeit for the first time, that one's girlfriend is ungainly. At other moments, certainly, these inferences would be small matters indeed; but in times of trouble, in times when one's inner gyroscope has gone haywire, the color of one's toothbrush looms like the greatest epiphany in the world. Good writers understand this: they suggest how life sluices into everything—how the sloppy ways of pain slosh into the hue of the day, the feel of the mist, the size of one's body. It is Flannery O'Conner who reminds us that a young girl's curse in a doctor's office can truly bring *revelation* to an old, self-satisfied bigot. Before the young lady's malediction that the small-minded Mrs. Turpin was "an old wart hog from Hell," Mrs. Turpin overworked her black sharecroppers, made disparaging comments about everyone—"Sometimes Mrs. Turpin occupied herself at night naming the classes of people"—and knew that she and her husband, Claud, would most certainly go to heaven. But that young lady's shrill, hate-filled statement started a mudslide of self-investigation, and even Mrs. Turpin found herself sensing, albeit from an angle as wildly peculiar as her previous utterances, that she might not be at the head of the heaven-bound; indeed, she might be found bringing up the rear, with all the riffraff, "the white-trash, clean for the first time in their lives, and bands of black niggers in white robes, and battalions of freaks and lunatics shouting and clapping and leaping like frogs."

Or one is reminded of John Cheever's wonderful story "The Enormous Radio," in which the purchase of a radio—such a small act—celebrates how a hoping-to-be middle-class couple learns about the *real* lives of those they would so like to emulate. At first, the radio performs marvelously, playing lovely classical music, but then it begins to gather static, ultimately broadcasting conversations from their neighbors' apartments. The couple, understandably, is taken aback: they want the radio to work; they do not want to learn about the horror, the broken marriages, the drunken orgies of those about them. But soon the radio is compulsively turned on at every opportunity, and the couple delights in pinpointing whose distress the radio is presently carrying. Their need, like the radio's conveyed need, is everywhere, thick and static.

I recount this because a few years ago I failed to acknowledge something that years of reading and teaching should have made second nature. That it had to do with the death of my brother is still small justification. I have known for many years that the most difficult thing is to accept one's own truth, whatever its involvements; by the same token, the acceptance of a reality does not place oneself beyond its sting. Indeed, if that were the case, no one would ever dare to love after that first great betrayal. And still lovers take the plunge—and I, caught in grief and self-delusion, would journey to Connecticut in July, three days after my brother's death.

In October 1982, I was thrilled to be invited to give a poetry reading as part of New London, Connecticut's Unity Day. Unity Day, to be held on July 17, was an elaborate celebration of the multirich, multifaceted life of the black community. As its coordinator's letter proudly announced, I was to share in a very expansive program, including a martial arts demonstration, a fashion show, a wealth of "uplift" messages, and a covey of local music and radio personalities, the diva of whom, at least in appellative hyperbole, was "Plastic Man."

I can't tell you how excited—and frightened—I was at this request. It was unusual for me to read to large numbers of people, and the Unity Day celebration would draw crowds in the thousands. More importantly, I would finally have the opportunity to address a large cross-section of *black* people, and not just college students but workers from New London's large submarine and hydroelectric plants.

As a university professor, I had been largely a "journal poet." Although I wrote about black people and I certainly *was* black, I hadn't taken my offering to the black community. Now, in truth, I would finally have to face my greatest fears. As an adolescent I had often tried to move beyond my middle-class background and its preoccupations. The Harlem prep-school kid, understandably, was the albino of albinos: a person whose own needy, self-infested anxiety only conspired to drive a community's axiomatic anxiety feverish. Whatever I was, I seemed forever to place myself in contradistinction to the rubric of things, and Harlem, like any sociopolitical construct, had sacred cows aplenty. I was often scared, frightened and terrified of Harlem; terrified, that is, of the power the ghetto held in my imagination and of the rituals and nuances I could only marvel at. Yet I never—and this is essential—felt other than black. To

67

live in Harlem and to see only the faintish glimpses of the lives lived there was my family's lot. My father and mother were both professionals; I attended the Collegiate School. Although my father, for most of his career, practiced in Harlem—in a crummy office on 146th Street—we certainly were not, no matter how much we were respected and even loved by the community, members of it. I remember how my mother would give the neighborhood kids presents on Christmas—something one could do in 1955—and how, at least then, such a gesture did not seem particularly quixotic. The kids, in fact, enjoyed their trinkets; they were happy to receive them. And indeed, I only began to sense how strange was my family's grafting to the community as I reached puberty. My mother's romantic gift idea was her admonition, certainly, of our peculiar station; yet her attempts at healing were, I would submit, successful since no one beat us up, at least among the kids we knew. And, considering the enormous chasm between our lives and those around us, this was no small achievement.

I should state that the notion of true class distinctions within the black community is a complex one. A nice house in Harlem is still a *Harlem* house; and people in the community, since they do live in America and understand what Americans say about Harlem, realize that to reside in Harlem is to proclaim, at least symbolically, your allegiance to pariahdom and second-classdom. To some of our neighbors we were probably considered crazy; to others, good Samaritans; to most, people who were just trying to live.

Once, when I was eleven, a group of kids wanted to steal my brother's basketball. Paul was about nine years old, gangly, and, for the last time in his life, soft-looking. The park was about sixty yards from our front door, and I would periodically look out the window to check on my brother. Suddenly, seeing ten kids massing around him, I quickly ran out of the house and approached the group. Although the kids were younger than me, their numbers made my position vulnerable. One of them, the group leader, was particularly boastful, telling Paul

68

that he was going to steal his ball and "kick his ass." Ordinarily, I would never fight someone two years my junior, and yet I strongly felt that a quick jab at this braggart would defuse this motley assemblage before things might turn ugly. Yet, as I made ready to hit the big-mouthed kid, I heard my mother's voice admonishing me not to fight, reminding me that I was older and was not to bully. Hearing her, I had to relent, even though my street sense told me that I should act, and act decisively.

In a few moments the kids did go away, without the basketball but uttering threats. Then, about an hour later, they returned with a few more bodies, some a head taller than myself, sporting bats, tire irons, and chains. Had I originally followed my first impulse, the battle might have ended after my first blow, but now Paul and I were in for it.

The big fight, thank goodness, never took place. A friend of mine, Rafael, one of the few Puerto Ricans then living in New York in the late 1950s, played by the rules and deftly cut the ringleader with a penknife, causing a slight trickle of blood to run down his arm. If the mob was quick to fight, it was also quick to exit. And as soon as one person realized that his legs might carry him away, legs were seen everywhere. In the 1950s, this muscle flexing was enough; now, of course, with cocaine and humankind's ever-rapacious desire for fratricide, we might all be dead or maimed. But in the 1950s, one still enjoyed a sense of ritual and measure; retreat was still an honorable alternative.

Unity Day actually fell two days before my brother's funeral, which, of course, no one could have anticipated. One can plan for most eventualities; death, however, is not one of them. Looking back, I really shouldn't have attempted the reading; I certainly wasn't up to it. But I honored the commitment, I trust, largely because it gave me something to do.

My brother's death came as a complete surprise. He hadn't been ill (or, at least, he hadn't been hospitalized for more than thirteen days before he died), and thus the mental preparation for death—if one can ever truly be prepared—was sorely lacking. There was my father's call, his broken inference that my brother was dying of alcoholism (Paul always used to drink a great deal; I sensed now how bottomless "great" was), my utter amazement, the dismal plane ride home, the hospital visits, and finally his death. If death was quick, grief was incremental; and I had yet to take it on.

The trip to New London was uneventful. It was a hot day, and Rochelle, my wife, listened as I deliberated over what I would read in a few hours. Thank goodness, she was far more in touch with reality than I was. I might not understand my utter dis-ease, but she, as my lover, knew what miles I had traveled. The strange thing about reality is that it tends to fool only those who think they have fooled it. And I was a fool's fool.

I had been asked to read for forty to fifty minutes, and so I dutifully jotted down the titles of fifteen poems. That morning all my poems seemed either too long or too dark. In truth, I have always wished that I wrote more humorous po-ems—poems, that is, which make the reader delight in the day instead of making the head hurt. Yet much of this self-flagellation, I trust, sprang from the difficulty of the hour, and the fact that even self-abuse is time-consuming. I do recall, yes, that I had on ugly black pants, which I had just purchased at Woolworth's for my brother's funeral. The pants were those horrible, elastic golfer's type, and though they tended to expand with one's movements, in the July heat they quickly became clammy. I had never liked black pants; I would never wear them again. How-ever, that day I sported them like a badge. At this point my brother's death had not yet truly involved me, and I could still perceive things as remote symbols of *someone else's* reality. Later on, his death would not permit me such distance, but I was still sleepwalking.

Upon our arrival in New London, we were driven to Ocean Beach Park by Mr. Jordan, the husband of Unity Day's organizer, Olena. The park—a lovely place—was situated on a long peninsula, jutting far out into the Atlantic Ocean, and I was amazed that a beach suitable for swimming could be found so close to a city. Discernibly, there were two continents of people:

one was enjoying the sun in the outdoor gazebo; the other was quietly sitting in a walled-in pavilion, listening to the scheduled presenters. Though it was merely eleven-thirty in the morning, the larger outdoor group had already consumed much beer and was having a ball. Three people were already smashed, waffling in that perilous zone between the sloppy vertical and the more certain horizontal. One man, who held four beers in his hand and was drinking from an open bottle of scotch, told me, as if it were the most natural thing in the world, that I should take off my pants. When I looked hesitant, he then showed me how, pulling his jeans off, one weedy leg after another. "It's too warm for those things, drop them," he yelled.

Since I was getting my usual prereading nervous stomach, Rochelle and I quietly entered the pavilion and awaited the beginning of James DeJonghn's play *Dear Lord Remember Me,* which was to begin in a few moments. However, when the stage curtains arose, we were confronted with a group of gospel singers, who, according to the program, were to have performed three hours earlier. Obviously, things were well off schedule; my reading, which was set to begin at twelve-thirty, in twenty minutes, would not begin until six or seven that evening. I was flabbergasted. Now I would have to cool my heels for another six hours.

I cannot overstate the importance of my wife's presence at this juncture. I had begun to *feel*—that is, I was now a grieving brother. And it was only Rochelle—by word, gesture, and careful prodding—who kept me together. Unobtrusively she'd take my hand and give me a slight smile; then, mysteriously, a cup of water or a can of soda would appear. She was there, simply *there*. And it seems odd that it is only now, at this writing, that I can fully relate this. I hope she is listening. I hope that love, then as now, is louder than my omnipresent, horrible silence.

While the gospel group performed, a young reporter from the *New London Leader* asked if he might interview me. I quickly agreed. His interview consisted of a twenty-minute discussion about books. The reporter had been an English major at Holy Cross, and I could sense his furious hunger to talk about poetry and fiction. I recall wondering how he managed to recollect any quotations, since he seemed rarely to write anything down. In my confusion, I must confess, I probably offered precious little worthy to report. Yet he still thanked me profusely, stating that he had to get back to the office to file his story. I thought it strange that he left so early but then surmised that he would write a short, general piece on the day's activities, casually mentioning some of the entertainment listed in the program. It was only the next morning, as my wife and I were busily leaving New London, that we would read his two-column article entitled "Cornell Poet Reads at Unity Day."

There is something invariably dreary about a people's commemoration. Such celebrations are usually the provender of those who have far too little to celebrate about. Those who have the world at their fingers rarely lionize themselves, since the reality that *you* work for *them* is recognition enough. Yet it remains the hapless province of the largely disenfranchised to honor whatever small accomplishments they can; and it is just this, which gives their festivals, jubilees, and the like that omnipresent aura of the wildly improbable and the patently desperate. Need is rarely artful; hunger even less so; and the desire to muzzle pain, if only for a moment, is as dubious a proposition as feeding water buffalo to a vegetarian.

Certainly, I don't mean to infer that Unity Day was a bad idea: it was an important idea, important largely because it was so desperately *needed*; and yet need of this sort—wide, unassimilable, central—cannot be dissembled; it can only be revealed. That black people have suffered is certainly not earthshaking to anyone, nor is it truly news that they have often suffered with grace, though this, of course, is less often recounted.

Still, the tale of a people's suffering is a pain-filled tale; one that is important because it *happened,* and because human beings faced it; but one, nonetheless, that is never pretty or upbeat. An ethnic celebration like Unity Day, no matter what its intention, can only be a sobering meditation on the human condition, much as a paraplegic—no matter how valiantly he or she has met her injustice—can only truly testify to the enormity of life's vicissitudes.

Finally, after a spirited fashion show, seven speeches, a mayoral proclamation, and three drill teams—not to mention the recognition of every person of note (or would-be note) in the city—it was unalterably my turn. As a member of the audience for the last six hours, I had heard far too many words to want to contribute any others. Indeed, as my hour drew nigh, I had, with Rochelle's encouragement, constantly trimmed my program. By the time I was actually to read, I had pruned my poems to three (and even that, I felt, was three too many).

The audience, understandably, had become increasingly restive. The sun was hot, there was much beer and booze, and "uplift," no matter how important, can only involve one for so long. My poems, frankly, were becoming addled fruit in my pocket; like an old pumpkin, they had soured at the center. Had I begun the program six hours earlier, then well-crafted lyrics about Judge Bruce Wright (meanly termed "Turn Them Loose Bruce" by his detractors) or Langston Hughes might have carried the day. But now, unless I were Gwendolyn Brooks, Eddie Murphy, or Aretha Franklin, I was in for trouble. These folks did not want to sit anymore; they wanted to *move.* And I wanted to join them.

At six, Mrs. Jordan, as master of ceremonies, began her generous introduction of "the professor who came all the way from Cornell University to share his distinguished verse." Before she could finish, the crowd had drowned her out. I had known women like Mrs. Jordan all my life. Enormously intelligent, strong, and resilient, she moved with an elegance as precise as it was unrehearsed, weaving in and out of circumstances, with that rich, almost offhand lightness of carriage that the dismissive have; but Mrs. Jordan was neither dismissive nor easygoing; and our inability to locate her was certainly not her inability to locate herself. The person we saw was not the person we intuited saw us; and that revelation, and the power it disclosed, carried us to the shores of wonder.

Still unruffled, Mrs. Jordan tried again to introduce me, and the crowd, for a few seconds, quieted. Yet before long she was again inaudible. Then, in the most graceful act of anger, Mrs. Jordan threw her hands up, slicing the air like a scythe. "This *was* a program. We should treat important guests with respect, especially if they have traveled all the way from upstate New York," she stated. And again the crowd grew quiet, but only momentarily. Now Mrs. Jordan looked over at us; she was tired, ashamed, and frustrated.

Suddenly, from the back of the pavilion, came a great deafening sound, much like a sonic boom. It was "Plastic Man," the hottest disc jockey in southeastern Connecticut, and he was ready to party. Yes, he had been scheduled for four o'clock, but, like the rest of us, he had waited too long, and it was time to jam. Grabbing the mike, he yelled, "Brothers and sisters, do you want to hear poetry or music? This is Plastic Man." And before anyone could answer, his macro-speakers again rumbled, shaking the beach, and probably all Earth and Mars. Now, obviously in control, Plastic Man threw on a Stevie Wonder cut, and Mrs. Jordan began to cry.

Rochelle and I went up to her, hoping that she would not try to outmatch Plastic Man. Mrs. Jordan muttered to me that she didn't feel that the crowd would listen to my poetry, and I agreed. I think she may have sensed how relieved I was, although she couldn't know the level of my previous despair. For Mrs. Jordan, this breach of decorum was unconscionable: the Race had floundered. For me, it was yet another peculiar interlude in a terribly disjointed time.

Although Rochelle and I had originally planned to leave New London the next morning, we now desperately wanted to get out of town. And incredibly, after numerous calls and inquiries, we could neither lease a car, locate a bus, nor purchase a plane ticket.

In truth, nothing that occurred on Unity Day was particularly disgruntling in itself. Certainly there was a good deal of negotiation and renegotiation, and I shall never forget Plastic Man, but that was not cause for cosmic alarm. I guess, in hindsight, that we were both responding to the awful displacement, the terrible confluence of events (both examined and unconscious) which had overtaken us. I may never fully understand what so gripped me to leave New London that night, but once the feeling had taken hold, it would not let go. The fact that there were no trains, no rental cars, and no buses only conspired to make our desire more profound and our despair more bottomless.

Finally, after a long, soothing talk with the Jordans, Rochelle and I accepted the incontrovertible and simmered down. We were going to spend the night.

The next day, after a fine breakfast with the Jordans— replete with ham, bacon, eggs, homemade rolls, grits, and stomachs that could not get any tighter—we were driven to the bus station for the long sojourn to my brother's funeral. For the trip Rochelle brought a candy bar and a newspaper. Among the headlines was an article about my "brilliant" poetry reading at Unity Day, which she read to me.

I thought about the poetry reading, Mrs. Jordan, Plastic Man, my family, and my late brother. I thought about the events of the last ten days, the events of the last twenty-four hours. I thought about my life and my would-be life. I thought about Rochelle. I thought about the nebulous terms *cause* and *effect,* and how my brother had slowly shrunk away from us, drinking alcohol and using heroin, playing the drums like some phantom, his forays into our world less and less pronounced, less and less noticed. I thought about a life which is unassimilable, which severs and does not repair, which takes a brother away like something barely visiting. I thought about my parents and that failure—real and imagined—which will be burned in them forever. I thought about our fights and the last time Paul called, telling me about his girlfriend who had left him "because he had nothing." I thought about the particularly hollow sound in his throat—something like a bird drowning or a door finally closed—and how that sound shall forever remind me of all that is unwell and sorrowful in the world. I thought about the time I went to protect his diminutive form, slowly escaping from me in the sea of those others—those who would be driven away, at least that day, in that city, which, for a small, precious time, permitted us each other.

Baxter's Program:
Creative Writing at Cornell

Could a greater miracle take place than for us to
look through each other's eyes for an instant?
—Henry David Thoreau

The first meeting of a creative writing seminar is always particularly exciting. There are the new students, their faces alternately open and grave, and a knife-edged, heady wind of expectancy. For this is a *writing* class, the world is to be revised and revisited; and everyone senses, from the initiate to the daily scribbler, that this is a miraculous event. Pearl Buck had once sat in these same seats, and so had Kurt Vonnegut. If such greatness began *somewhere* and with *someone*, it was not unreasonable to believe that it might happen, yes, even here, to someone in *this* room. And so the first class invariably bristles with the suggestion of journey, of magic. Sadly, the wages of talent and passion will soon take their measure; but on this day, this first day, we are all marvelously equal.

I write here, of course, from experience. I too was once a student, sitting in Goldwin Smith Hall, finding my poems discussed, praised, and amended. Though it was fifteen years ago, I still remember Professor Baxter Hathaway—thin and white-haired—telling me, "McClane, you're really not all that bad," when I most needed to hear it.

At that time I had begun to let the world's seeming indifference consume me: I had lost my bravado, my I-can-do-anything-and-the-world-be-damned attitude. And Baxter sensed this. Like all great writing teachers, he knew the difference between a writer's hope for praise (something axiomatic) and his need for absolute confirmation, which involves a writer's *life*.

From Baxter, any statement beyond censure was approbation. For Baxter didn't mince words; he didn't celebrate the peripheral; he kept his standards unwaveringly. And yet, like all the remarkable teachers who would join his writing program— Archie Ammons, Walter Slatoff, Edgar Rosenberg, Anthony Caputi, Alison Lurie, Robert Morgan, Phyllis Janowitz, James McConkey, Stephanie Vaughn, Lamar Herrin, and Dan McCall— he loved writers and writing. No one who studied with him would ever forget how powerfully Baxter believed that writing was the "highest" profession, something sacred and inviolable.

Indeed, if Baxter was hard on us, he was unmercifully so on himself. Baxter had written hundreds of poems and two novels, all of which he would unceremoniously term "drivel." If we were to write, we were to write well. And Baxter would remain at the gate, pushing, elevating, tempering, making us writers of more than just "small" pleasures. He was fond of saying that the world could not abide another "minor poet." And to him, and to us, to be relegated to such a position was like acquiescing to leprosy.

Often Baxter would decry the state of the culture, but, like most of my ilk, I was too caught in my own eddies to understand his concern. The young may be vital, but they are rarely generous. The cry of their omnipresent genes—that marvelous chemical catechism that will not be silenced— outmaneuvers the wisdom of much else. Baxter's sorrow was Baxter's trouble, or so we then thought. If the culture didn't care about poetry, *we* certainly did. And *we*, yes, were all that mattered.

Now, as a teacher, I understand Baxter's distress all too well. For whatever the joys of watching a young writer's evolution, the world is a brutal place. Even if a student is truly gifted—and many of my students are—there is little cause for celebration. One knows far too many writers—good writers—who have fallen by the wayside. One sees them in the bars, in the streets. One sees them working horrible hours, sojourning with the slimmest hope of a career, their eyes not yet hardened, their imaginations slowly idling, beginning that awful calculus. For it is not too long before the world's contempt invites their own, when they, themselves, become mere husks, doomed scaffolding.

It is a terrible thing to watch a dream collapse; more terrible, indeed, when the dream is so terribly needed—and not only by the dreamer. And that was what Baxter was so desperately trying to tell us. He wanted us to write, and he wanted us to live, and he knew that talent, however rich, might not protect us.

Still, a true writer can't easily turn writing off; it's in the blood, and one does enormous damage to oneself, the human spirit, and the fragile balance of everything if one does not take it seriously. If writing is pain-filled, risky, and often futureless, it is also confirming, intoxicating, and liberating. Writers are simply hardheaded. They *will* write, no matter what the cost.

The writing seminar is a strange congress, part a course in the rudiments of a discipline—questions of style, metrics, form—and part a far more difficult and at times precipitous undertaking. In a creative writing class, the easiest questions are those of technique: a villanelle observes this convention; the selective omniscient narrator permits a story this range of effect. But the *real* work demands that teacher and student become vulnerable in a way that few welcome. The teacher must remember that he or she is a "professional" writer, and not everyone in the seminar wishes to be or, Lord knows, needs to be. The students, on the other hand, must begin the difficult process of discovering what indeed they can use to fuel their art, and that is by no means a simple proposition. Life and art are difficult soul mates: the demands of one are often the scourge of the other.

All this may sound somewhat dreary, but in my eleven years teaching here, both young writers and teachers have

prospered. The creative writing courses have grown exponen-
tially. In 1976, we offered merely a handful of creative writing
classes. This fall, there are thirteen sections of introductory
creative writing, four sections of intermediate writing (two in
poetry and two in prose), and two sections of the senior writing
seminar. And still we turn hundreds of students away. In the last
five years I have taught two national poetry prize winners, six
practicing editors, seven published novelists, and literally
hundreds of sane, decent human beings who found writing
personally invaluable.

The faculty, too, has grown. When I first began teaching here, Cornell had six full-time writers; now we have twelve.
There have been prizes—Alison Lurie's Pulitzer, Archie
Ammons's National Book Award, James McConkey's Academy
of American Arts and Letters Award—and there has been a
nearly incomprehensible output of books.

Although no one can teach someone to become a
William Faulkner, a James Baldwin, or an Emily Dickinson, one
can suggest an attitude toward writing, experience, and self that
is sustaining and provident. Each of us has something essential
to relate, however tentative. At Cornell, we are not so much
concerned with creating wan imitations of Shakespeare as we
are with aiding the difficult announcements of each individual
who tries his or her hand at writing. Shakespeare did not try to
be Chaucer; Susan should not wish to be John. And thus, all of us
who teach try our damnedest to permit our students their own
voices and involvements. It means something to be born in
Georgia or India, something to have grown up in the hills of
North Carolina or the streets of Harlem, something indissolubly
wondrous and crucial.

And yet art and circumstance are not interchangeable.
It is not enough to state that I, for example, grew up on 147th
Street in Manhattan, in a brownstone, with a young brother who
would later kill himself. These facts, however painful, are not
the *essential* story. The true narrative celebrates how these
forces acted upon *me*: how I, a unique individual, and yet

someone with the same fears, aspirations, and passions as others, confronted something inescapable, employing what powers of spirit I could muster.

Writing, ultimately, is a public act. However much one argues otherwise—and there are many who do—writing is, at bottom, a projection from a self to *other* selves. If one wishes to write for oneself, one keeps a journal. But the act of placing one's thoughts before another signifies an implied commitment, a celebration of interdependence. The writer, like a lover, cannot casually disavow the reader's feelings or demands; the reader, understandably, wants his or her involvement acknowledged. For once I become interested in *your* story, it becomes *my* story. And in these terrible times, when one tenaciously avoids self-revelation and commitment, such authorial treachery—if I may term it that—is not only irresponsible, it is unconscionable, for it strikes at our most precious human gift: our willingness to become interconnected.

At the outset of each semester I tell my creative writing students, to their great astonishment, I am certain, that I know I am capable of murder. I do this not to scare them, although the notion continues to scare me. I tell them this because I want them to understand the importance of vulnerability and honesty.

Once, when I was young, I threw a dart at my brother and narrowly missed puncturing his heart. Certainly I didn't intend to kill him; I wasn't thinking that clearly. But the truth remains incontrovertible: *I might have killed my brother.*

I make this admonition, again, because I want my students to understand that the realization that I was capable of something so personally frightening and repugnant as murder necessitated that I face the world anew, realizing that with human beings all things are possible, and that I could no longer rely upon the easy assurances of what was humanly possible for me. If I intended never to hurt someone, I would have to struggle eternally never to do so.

Importantly, this self-realization had a welcomed side effect: it made me generous. For as I had to accept my own difficult humanity, so too did I have to acknowledge others' human frailty. I had to look at them, as I had to look at myself, as a vast spiritual conundrum, capable of love and destruction. And as I tell my students, from that moment I became, in attitude, a writer.

At Cornell, I'm not certain that we have produced more Thomas Pynchons or E. B. Whites than other places, but we have supported many who, at least for the moment, have found the inner life special and ineludible. I remember Scott Sommer, author of five Random House novels, and Alice Fulton, winner of the Associated Writing Program's Poetry Prize for her splendid book *Dance Script with Electric Ballerina*; I also remember Vernon Jackman, who wrote lovely lyrics about his native Barbados; and hundreds of other students—talented students—who wanted to be everything but writers: lawyers, doctors, anthropologists. Many of them, on the strength of their talent, would have been fine writers, possibly even great ones. But talent and desire, like love and fortune, do not always dance together.

If experience is any indication, my students will run mightily at life. They will do out in the world what they did here: they will think well, argue well, and live responsibly. If few actually become writers, I trust all will remember that the violence of life is real violence; that each of us is important, sacred, and menaced; and that there is no greater human virtue than mercy.

For if writing teaches us anything, it confirms that we are *wonderfully and fearfully made*. It suggests that my terror is your terror; my love is your love; the world that frightens me frightens you.

As Baxter Hathaway so desperately tried to teach me fifteen years ago, there is no safety in lies, in self-righteousness, in disengagement: the world—plain and simple—is not *safe*. To fancy it so is to do more than mangle reality; it is to place oneself and others in peril.

Intimate Injustice

A few days ago I was offered a whopping one hundred and fifty thousand dollars for our summer home on the island of Martha's Vineyard. Even though the house was not mine to sell—it belongs to my parents—the figure seemed out of all proportion to reality.

Undeniably, the house is a grand one. With ten rooms, a lovely porch (designed by the architect of the Panama Canal, Thomas Goethals), a palatial sun room, and a wonderful, if sometimes elusive, view of the Oak Bluffs Harbor, it is a setting worthy of Monet. I wrote my first poem while looking out from the sun room, watching the wind stir the lilac; my mother painted her prize-winning "Day at Length" there. As with all things, one's memories are either bitter or sweet, depending on the freight of the imagined and the thirst of the imaginer.

Yet, no matter what its charm, the house is a summer cottage—with no heat, little insulation, and a general airiness. In the eighty-five-degree summer heat, one can delight in the wind whipping through its porous walls as if they were mosquito netting; in the winter, however, these same walls act like a deadly sieve, the damp, moist air rushing like water through a parched field.

83

My parents actually bought the house in 1943 for twenty-five hundred dollars, after my father had been practicing medicine for three years. At that time he and my mother went for broke. With little but the arrogance of love, they scraped together the funds, spending every penny they had. In 1947, after seeing the wonderful Lerner and Lowe musical, they christened the house "Brigadoon," replete with a champagne party. If anything, the house was a place thatched out of dreams and wonder—at least for them. Like the enchanted country in the musical, our cottage seemed to rise out of the mist, wondrous in its apparition, recalling, at least for my parents, the only time when they cast discretion to the winds. Never again would they so resolutely trust their intuition; never again would they be so young, care-free, and sassy.

If the sum of one hundred and fifty thousand dollars seemed remarkable, even more so was the fact that I thought of accepting it. This house had once been a symbol of unbridled fun and delight; now it rankled like a broken rib.

My parents, certainly, did not view the Vineyard house as I did. They, for their own understandable reasons, tenaciously clung to the joy-laden past which salved the present. The Vineyard had once been a euphoric place for them: they remembered the gala beach parties; the gay times with the children; the brilliant overturning of a racist ordinance then prohibiting blacks from playing golf at the "public" country club; the giddy love they made in the upstairs bedroom; the long trips in broken-down cars from New York City to the island, one with war-issue tires so flimsy they exploded every twenty-five miles; the early-morning light which crept up the trellis like a hand opening; and the eerie soul-hungry drone of the East Chop foghorn, wailing like a loon to the distant Indian shores of Squibnocket, Tashmoo, and Wampannog.

Yet, for my part, the present was unavoidable: it was my only *reality*. And thus my parents' reminiscences about the glorious past seemed but idle talk. All I could connote with the Vineyard was my dead alcoholic brother and my sister Adrienne, who—in her long, lonely sojourn—showed me the island's hind parts.

It is a much exploited notion that places cannot be divorced from the people who make them up, and Martha's Vineyard is no exception. Largely a resort community (or, at least, that is what the vacationers and the monied people like to think), the island is also inhabited by fishermen, artists, carpenters, and craftspeople—the *real* folk, if you will. For many years, with various levels of difficulty, the vacationers and the true islanders (the "natives," as they are called) have coexisted, with the proportion (the ratio between native to summer visitor) the most interesting variable. Thirty years ago, the island had a small winter population and an equally tiny summer influx. Recently, however, with the advent of the "jet-setters"—such personages as Carly Simon, James Taylor, and Walter Cronkite—the island has become the place to go. Now the island's winter community is numbered about twelve thousand, while the summer community swells to fifteen times that. Naturally, the delicate equilibrium has been affected.

My sister, who is now fifty and is handicapped, grew up on the island. She first visited when my parents bought the house in a mad two-day house-hunting session. There is a long story concerning the house's purchase—one that also explains my parents' penchant for "Brigadoon," the name which, incidentally, they painted on a life preserver—but its gist is that the neighbors did not want a "colored" family entering their midst. Initially, when the real estate broker showed my parents the house, he was most accommodating; then, after he sensed the neighbors' growing opposition, he quickly reneged. In less time than it takes to spell the word *family*, my parents threatened to sue the Realtor and the town. In two days, we had thrust our way into East Chop.

In truth, the transition was far from bloody. The neighbors, thank goodness, were really not die-hard bigots; they were just foolish, isolated people. In a few weeks, they realized that the black family were good people, and that having a physician, no matter what his color, was not a bad thing, especially in a remote, out-of-the-way place.

One family, however, could not make the adjustment. Their house—a large red one—sat right behind ours on the Monday we moved in; by Wednesday, we were amazed to see a great bare spot—a giant wound—where the house had once stood. Instead of making peace with us, these people moved their entire ten-room domicile, leaving only the barest suggestion that human beings had once resided there: a red and white tricycle. It seemed both funny and sad, laughable and dreary.

Once we were settled in, my sister quickly made friends with our neighbors. To them she was a wonderful child. Indeed, her enormous openness and wanderlust made her the ideal peace offering. She did not, as my parents did, remember the neighbors' prior acts of nullification; she saw only their present plentiful acts of friendliness—the offer of candy, the help to set her bike chain back on its sprocket, the ready lemonade. In many ways, Adrienne's disinclination to judge, which is at the center of her personality, permitted the neighbors the opportunity to reclaim their bedraggled humanity. And whatever else my parents felt, they could not casually dismiss the many acts of kindness extended to their child.

My sister's handicap was acquired when she was born and did not breathe for twelve minutes. That day, my father, the parent-doctor, eagerly watched the cesarean birth from the upstairs hospital observation deck, and literally passed out when he realized that his first child was not inhaling and there was nothing he could do about it. The problem was that my mother had been overanesthetized. In those days, there was no safe intravenous anesthetic, which could be monitored; surgery was done by gas. In truth, my sister was unconscious from the moment the ether took hold. When she finally breathed, after constant striking, her small frame came to life with a start. As my father remembers, Adrienne did not cry; she merely whimpered, her tiny ribs moving like a broken accordion.

It was good that my father was not the attending obstetrician: it is horrible enough to watch your child suffer; it would have been unbearable to be the one who, slap after slap, couldn't make this silent thing open up and take in the world. This, thank goodness, did not befall my father, although each slap, I know, resounds eternally in his head.

Adrienne, thereafter, has always been mentally under-developed, though our understanding of this, with time and situation, has changed. Indeed, in many ways, her predicament only accentuated the fact that she was a unique individual. In theory, we proclaim that each of us is particularized at birth: each has specific talents, abilities, looks. But in Adrienne's case, her birth—and its attendant difficulties—presaged a specialized tale, the contents of which only Adrienne might tell us. For brain damage affects everyone differently. It can make its impact felt all at once, at birth; or it can weave in and out of a person's life, touching down here and there, like a vengeful bee. Whatever the case, there are people whose love will be mightily tested: parents, brothers and sisters, the mentally handicapped person himself or herself.

In my sister's case, Adrienne at first appeared normal. In her first six years my parents found themselves believing that the awful oxygen deprivation had somehow brought no ill effects. Yet after age six, Adrienne no longer kept pace with her peers; she, for all intents and purposes, just stopped developing. Her body would grow—she would become a tall, shapely woman of five feet, eleven inches—but her mind would remain forever locked in its six-year-old world. And this, indeed, was the horror. For although a six-year-old can be unusually discrimi-nating at times, she cannot—and this is essential—fully inte-grate cause with effect, feelings with needs, wishes with respon-sibility. My sister—at least until recently—could be counted on to read the newspaper, to discuss in some detail what she had read, and to prepare her own food. Yet she could never be left alone in the house, since she would routinely leave the door unlocked or neglect to turn off the stove. In New York, I can well remember seeing the door fly open, only to watch some young hood beginning his climb to our bedrooms. We lived in Harlem, and I had reason for terror. I recall, my heart wildly pumping, chasing him down the steps and into the street. I don't know what I looked like that day—I must have been a sight!—but my fear and anger scared even that intrepid interloper.

Adrienne's history with the oven was little more promising. Although with supervision she could easily prepare her own breakfast and lunch, she seemed hell-bent on leaving the stove on. Repeatedly I would find the gas jet partially turned off—which was far more dangerous than leaving it completely turned on. The chance of a fire caused by an open gas vent was not negligible; but it paled in comparison to the tragedy of a family totally asphyxiated, the invisible gas fumes everywhere. These lapses were not intentional by any means, and Adrienne was always apologetic. Still Adrienne, as she grew older, would smoke in bed; and my mother, terribly frightened, would encounter burn hole after burn hole in my sister's sheets.

Yet in the early years of our Vineyard stays, Adrienne was welcomed in the community. I remember how everyone recognized her, how they always saw her walking and delighted in her ubiquity. Many of the neighbors would offer her small jobs to do; she was always invited in to chat, especially by the older people who found her lack of guile refreshing.

Adrienne, at that time, had her own friends. She was still—I'm speaking here from the age of eight to twelve—miscible with others. She swam, biked, and went to parties; people often came to the house to visit. Although she was clearly different from her peers, they liked her. At that age her friends were less judgmental: too caught up in their own desperate attempts to forge a self, they could not pay much attention to the apparent frailty of someone else. Thus, for a brief period, their self-absorption was a peculiar godsend, and Adrienne had a wonderful time.

Sadly, this was the last time Adrienne truly felt part of the world. Indeed, it was during this period that Adrienne made her one great friend, Cheryl Thomas, who remained close to Adrienne all her life. Cheryl would later die from sickle-cell anemia, and my sister would lose her only confidant. Yet while Cheryl was alive, she continued to visit and to write to Adrienne for twenty-five years. With the exception of my immediate family, Cheryl was the only person who thought of Adrienne as other than a waif. And Cheryl's friendship—which provided Adrienne with her only regular community—was as touching, sacred, and undiminishable as any the world has ever known.

One, in this age of cynicism, is tempted to suggest that Cheryl's generosity reflected her own precarious state, for Cheryl knew that she was terminally ill for most of her forty-three years. Yet if this had any real bearing, it mattered little in the range and power of the love she held for Adrienne and Adrienne held for her. For me, there were precious few times when I understood what my sister truly perceived; her gift of a wonderful friend was one of these. I thank Cheryl today for her love; I thank her for showing me my sister's great capacity for joy, for never again would Adrienne appear so loose with laughter.

As time passed and Adrienne grew older—her body always enlarging, her girlishness remaining constant—the same actions that had once solicited praise or mild curiosity from others became cause for fear and censure. In New York and Martha's Vineyard, Adrienne was now considered a problem. The island community—with the exception of a precious few— could no longer see the girl-child in the woman's body. A child is a child, and one, almost instinctively, permits a child a certain field of action: a child can shout, cry, take her clothes off. A woman, however, "must put away childish things"; she must live within a certain ambit of decorum. Yet Adrienne, however much she looked like a woman, was not a woman. She might, on a hot day, take down her halter, not because she coveted the attentions of men (as was rumored) but because she was simply *hot.* Or, feeling sociable, Adrienne might walk into a bar—after all, she was fifty years old, and people her age *do* drink—and imbibe ten beers, with disastrous consequences.

The policeman, the neighbor, and the citizen see only the woman who has transgressed the law, one who must be punished, even banished if need be. Yet Adrienne was merely trying to survive to the best of her abilities. When she was hot, she did what was natural to cool herself and took off a piece of clothing; in the bar, trying to act as she had seen others do in the commercials, she downed a few beers. Clearly, Adrienne did not think of the consequences; she did not know what they were.

Now, I am not trying to suggest that I fail to understand society's difficulty with Adrienne's actions. I know all too well the problems; my family has lived with them all too long. Yet I do believe that she deserves better than countless arrests and prosecutions; I would hope that the world might see in her what I would hope it sees in me: an indomitable spirit trying to make its presence felt.

My sister is not mean, dangerous, or crazy; she is, however, frustrated. She wants, I think, what we all want, although she is less inclined to distinguish between different brands of clothing—*a hat is, after all, a hat*—and I have never known her to make a distinction between bars, other than to frequent places that are kind to her. And that, I think, is all too human.

As I suggested earlier on, mental retardation has its own progression. For Adrienne, the process has been one long, slow sting. When she was in her twenties she worked in a hospital, washing dishes. But a vicious coworker, desiring to hire a friend, told my sister that her job would be lost if she did not agree to a blood test. This coworker knew that my sister had always been terrified of needles, indeed of anything medical. Adrienne would not take injections; she would never go to the doctor; if she was ever ill, all the antibiotics had to be given to her by mouth. Indeed, this fear of doctors caused Adrienne to suffer many painful maladies. Often my father would notice Adrienne limping; yet it was only after ceaseless pestering that she would show him her infected feet. So, sadly, this coworker literally deceived my sister into resigning. In point of fact, there was no actual blood test to be taken; my sister, in her fear, simply told her supervisor that she was quitting. For her part, the supervisor did little to push Adrienne for an explanation; she, too, must have been in on the scheme. Tragically, this was the last time Adrienne ever worked. It was her last pretext of societal connection.

Of late, Adrienne has started to dress like a bag woman, her manner becoming, if you will, the metaphor for society's seemingly aboriginal abandonment. Adorning herself with an elaborate repertoire of outfits—swimsuits over woolen coats, two pair of slacks worn over each other, anything and everything—Adrienne seems flagrantly to parody her position of pariah. Often she goes begging for quarters, even if she has money—and my parents give her a daily allowance. In these wild outfits, and in her constant panhandling, Adrienne, in fact, has made guerrilla theater of her life. People who would not speak to her when she was as "normal" as she could be speak to her now in repulsion and contempt. And yet their invectives are, in truth, what they have always secretly believed—the secret kept, because they, at least to that point, were not hurled into honesty.

Almost imperceptibly, Adrienne, like all the world's historically damned, would inhabit the place proffered her. Much like Sula in Toni Morrison's wonderful novel, Adrienne would become the repository for all the world's ills; but not easily, not without a sense of hate and outrage, not without a wish for revenge.

For Adrienne, it seems to me, has become a symbol—albeit a horrific one—of her torment *and* tormentors. Now she is begging for money she does not need; before, she was begging for the love she did. The implications, I think, are obvious: like any symbol, Adrienne mirrors her creators; and it is we—who would not bring her into the human family, who cast her out—who are confronted with this grotesque of our own invention. In the eyes of one's victim one sees oneself.

In New York, where there is room for everyone and

everything, Adrienne has quietly entered the great community of the fallen. For in the Great City, there is ample evidence of the world's leveling: everyone knows and sees the ravages of suffering; everyone, more importantly, understands the narrow gossamer wall between the world's blessed and the world's cursed; everyone, each and every day, sees the slow slippage of his or her friends and work mates; everyone knows how thinly he or she has escaped the bread line, the mental ward, the detoxification unit.

Yet on Martha's Vineyard, where people still proclaim, however disingenuously, that a beautiful island bespeaks beautiful people, Adrienne's bedraggled demeanor is a blight. To see her wearing three coats, her hair unkempt, is to be reminded that there is no possible true escape, that the world's mire is everywhere. The Vineyard vacationers, it must be remembered, pay a tremendous price for their Shangri-la. The island is difficult to achieve by any mode of transportation. If you drive, you must wind your way to the tip of Cape Cod and then take a forty-five-minute ferry trip, which is both costly and vexing. If you travel by plane, you are met by an imperious nature. During the summer, the shore breezes, like a demonic child, waft in great globs of fog, and often the plane cannot land. Undeniably, it is no overstatement to suggest that getting to the Vineyard is truly a hellish experience. And so to justify one's endless aggravation—for pain, of course, needs a poultice—the aggrieved further mythologize the island. In this myth, of course, there are no weeds, no disappointments, no Adriennes.

All of this, unquestionably, has been terribly damaging to my parents, who, no matter what the present turn of events, very much love their daughter. In truth, they have kept her at home at great psychological expense. My brother's death, to some degree, I think, might be laid at the foot of my sister's presence; much strain, certainly, has been part of the family. And yet my parents were not willing to place Adrienne in an institution in the 1940s, when they were horrendous; the institutions now, although much better, are too expensive.

Now at age seventy-five, my mother and father are terribly tired; Adrienne is too much for them to handle. It is clear to me that she is beyond them; it is clear to them, when they are not trying to be stoic, that they need help. The hardest thing, I think, is that my parents, however obliquely, want a human presence about them. I am living far away from them in Ithaca, New York; my brother is dead. Adrienne, whatever her frustrations, is still their child. And they, like anyone, wish to be needed, to be loved.

Sadly, of course, *their* need is no longer in the best interests of Adrienne. Her retardation is degenerative; she will become more and more remote, more and more truculent. Surely, there is little doubt they can keep her much longer; at age fifty, Adrienne is formidable, strong, and athletic, and my parents are fragile, imaginatively overwrought, and retiring.

Recently, Adrienne has been seen eating garbage, though she has plenty of good food to eat at home. Twice she has even been physically abusive to my parents, once hitting my mother in the head with a garbage can. These altercations, thank goodness, are rare. Yet they are undeniable harbingers of a terrible future.

Now when my parents visit the Vineyard in June, the police have developed a plan for Adrienne, which keeps the island community happy. As soon as she hits the island, Adrienne is arrested, taken to the Dukes County Court House, and delivered to Pocasset, the state sanitarium in Taunton, Massachusetts, where she remains until my parents pick her up on their way back to New York City in September.

I have often witnessed this mockery of a trial. Adrienne is brought before the judge, asked a few questions, and then remanded to the state. What is so touching is that Adrienne becomes terribly sober and attentive in the courtroom. When interrogated, she answers in a solemn voice, and seems wondrously engaged, as if the high seriousness of the event has particular meaning for her. Sometimes she wears a pretty blue smock, with a lovely embroidered neck; at other times, whatever we can scare up. Always, the prettiness of her cheekbones—the same ones that grace my mother—become pronounced, and her face shows both the fury and the ease that alternately explain her.

During the six minutes of this constitutional charade, my sister is truly resplendent: finally, she has gleaned that so much needed attention. Adrienne, for some reason, smiles—almost like a bemused gnome—and I am carried back to when she was eleven, and the world was all possibility. And then, just before she is led away, she inevitably looks at me rather sheepishly, as if we shared a large, weighty secret.

In these court battles, my parents and I are placed in a terrible quandary. We know that Adrienne is beyond us and that we can no longer help her; we also know—and this stings like a fish hook—that the System only wishes to banish this temporary ugliness from its quaint streets.

At no time has anyone dealt adequately with my sister. She has moved through our corridors of power; she has been ridiculed and demoralized; she has been lied to. Lately I haven't returned to the Vineyard with much frequency: I go there only to see my parents, and my sister, if they haven't yet sent her to the state's closet.

There's something so ugly in the state's musical chairs with Adrienne, as if it were some cosmic game. I don't know what her personal pain is when confronting this horror. I only know she misses us when she is taken away, and begs to come with us when we visit her weekly at Pocasset.

Adrienne moves through our world like a whale: our harpoons gouging her flesh, her silence a further incitement to pick, hurt, and disavow. I know that what we have done to Adrienne is what we have done to blacks, Native Americans, Jews, and women—to anyone who is different. I also know that it is romantic to believe that human empathy is commonplace, since empathy demands connection, and connection demands that one take on the burden of another's life, another's suffering.

I think my parents were not merely being quixotic to name the Vineyard house "Brigadoon," since, as you recall, they did not stop there. The name was affixed to a life preserver—one of the old heavy cork kind, which came from an ocean tug—and was hung on a tree beside the porch. For my parents, Brigadoon—a belief in a magical place—could act as a life ring, an amulet. And yet if my parents were paying obeisance to Shangri-la, they were also placating spirits darker, more exacting, more fundamental, spirits that tore and rent asunder. Obviously, this had everything to do with their life, their daughter, and their intimate injustice, with their realization that things happen—horrible things, unspeakable things—to you and to me.

Keep On Keeping On

I am on my way—I'm coming through.
—James Baldwin

I met the great writer James Baldwin on three very singular occasions: once when he gave a lecture and signed my copy of *Just Above My Head*; a second time when he and I had a drink together in Ithaca, New York; and a third time, when he was beyond all this, at his funeral at the Cathedral of St. John the Divine in New York City.

The first encounter remains the least memorable, since I was then, as I am now, terribly shy and self-conscious. I do recall that Baldwin was wearing a black leisure suit, with a wonderful purple ascot, and a wide-brimmed, floppy tam; but what most struck me—along with his infamous globe-sized eyes—was the fragility of his presence. Here was a man who appeared to be all bones and eyes, as if an erector set had gone crazy. Irreproachably dapper, there was also an extraordinary tentativeness in Baldwin's manner, as if he had just remembered this engagement and had arrived in the nick of time. Baldwin was known to miss commitments because he was characteristically overextended. Neither irresponsible nor dishonorable, he simply could not say no to anything if he felt his presence was needed, which provoked, as you can well imagine, the most vexatious of schedules. In fact, if you wanted Baldwin to appear at a certain time and place, you hastened to be the last person who held his attention, for Baldwin went where last asked. That he came to Cornell at all was because of the enormous dedication of Eleanor Traylor, one of Baldwin's dearest friends; and even she, ten minutes before he was to arrive at the Ithaca airport, worried that he might not be on the plane.

I don't know what I expected when I finally saw Baldwin. I guess I wanted a man larger than life, someone *significant*-looking, someone magisterial. Then again, I really don't know what I desired. Had he been ten feet tall, he would not have been monumental enough; had he spoken in tongues, dispensing the wisdom of ages, I would have been astonished but not appeased. One's imaginary connection with a favorite writer is a near sacred coupling: if it has much to do with the writer, it has everything to do with oneself; and in the strange symbiosis enacted here, two minds and two hearts really do become one. Yet this pairing, just as importantly, depends largely on the fact that the pleasure of one's private reading need not be defended, that one extracts from a book what one wishes, in the safety of one's own home, without the writer's interference. Yet when one encounters the book's creator in the flesh, things come unglued: the writer may not agree with the reader's reading; the author may have moved on to new themes or recanted the old ones; more treacherously, the author may accent elements the reader had conveniently overlooked or submerged, making it impossible for the reader to feel so irrepressibly, delightedly conjoined. The writer in the flesh, then, is all too human, all too difficult, all too demanding, and all too dangerous.

Like most people, Baldwin came as he came: his rage or pleasure took its measure from the shape of his bones, the inexpugnable insult of his flesh, the loping, easy carriage that was his way of moving in the world. And still, it was hard to imagine that *he*—this small, wiry head with bones—was the writer of *Another Country* and *The Fire Next Time*; hard to square this oceanic vulnerability with that volcanic prose which evidenced more than a token acquaintance with the world's chaos;

hard and not so hard, for Baldwin's physical softness under-scored his strength, if *strength* indeed is the proper word for something so unimpeachably apocalyptic in its refusal to be assertive.

Crucially, it was not what one saw but what one didn't see that was of importance here; and seeing nothing but this small man with his bubble eyes, who spoke the King's English with a venomous precision, one knew that revelation was upon us. Nothing Baldwin said or did conveyed this; but there was an irrefutable urgency in the room, like the screeching of all the world's wheels.

Baldwin on our first meeting, as I recall, was reading from *Sonny's Blues*, one of the world's great stories, and one which has particular importance for me. At twenty-nine, my brother Paul drank himself to death, and it was Baldwin's novella that permitted me to live, to forgive myself. I had felt terribly guilty about Paul's death. I was two years Paul's senior, and he and I had shared everything, including a love for conflict. Paul and I would argue about music and politics, druids and cheese. He would want this and I that; we could even find disagreement over the amount of soy sauce one brought home from the Chinese take-out.

But Paul's arguments tended to be silent ones: a slight swagger or nod of the head signified everything; he simply wouldn't talk. Once, when he was truly undone, he glared at me for ten minutes, without ever uttering a word. Indeed, it was the profoundest silence I had ever heard; the silence at the begin-ning of the world could not have been greater. So you can well understand how surprised I was when Paul had begun to call me almost daily at my home in Ithaca, New York.

At that time Paul lived with my parents in Harlem, with all its attendant frustrations. Along with house painting, Paul had been playing his drums here and there, but he really wasn't making any money, in a city that was brutally expensive. My parents worried about my brother; he worried about himself. They knew Paul was "marking time," but they couldn't imagine what he might do next, or what his dreams were. And yet the fact that Paul was living at home—even at age twenty-nine—was better than fearing him lost in the streets. Harlem is a killing machine: kids perish every day from hunger, from crack, from dreams gone crazy, from love, from want of love.

My parents, however much they worried about Paul, knew that Paul lived upstairs. He could be found—often sloppily drunk, often funky—but *found*, nonetheless. He would not end up freezing on 137th Street, or taking cocaine in the dark recesses of the subway platform, or bilking old ladies out of their meager welfare checks, or, most horribly, jumping off the George Washington Bridge, the cool wind kissing his thighs, like Baldwin's Rufus in *Another Country*.

These things happened every day, to all too many kids—all of whom had parents who cared—who *loved* them— but could do little to ensure their children's safety. "The city is a dying place," Aretha Franklin sings, and it is. No one could blame my parents for holding on to their son; no one could blame any parent for attempting anything in this sorrowing world. Parents tried; their children grew more remote; and there was always more death. This is why people in the ghetto rarely judge one another: there is simply too much injustice, too much failing, too much unassailable misfortune.

Paul was a very fine drummer. Over the years he had played with Carmen McCrae and Anthony Jackson. Just before his death, he had worked weekends in some of the most frightening—and most illustrious—jazz clubs in Harlem. Inevitably, the more funky-looking the club, the better the musicians who frequented it, and Paul had made every hole-in-the-wall his haunt. One of the clubs he particularly liked, Sam's Place, had watermarks decorating the walls and three famed bullet holes (*at-mos-phere*, its owners proudly called it), where one of the patrons had temporarily forgotten the quiet arts of compromise. Yet Sam's Place still remained a great hangout for musicians, since, unlike so many nightspots, it loved you when you were rich or on the skids. Paul would go there after he had played a few gigs and had some money; he would be there, when he hadn't played in months.

For the past five years, Paul had been dating a very lovely woman, who was the only truly bright spot in his life. Like so many others in the ghetto, Paul had first started to drink heavily; then it was on to grass; soon he was trying everything short of shooting up. Marsha loved Paul; she wanted him to love himself; then and only then might he be able to love her.

Paul, like all addicts, was drowning within himself: the things one previously prized about him—his fearlessness, his buoyancy, his ticklish yet unbridled sense of humor—quickly became menacing and self-parodic. I remember how he would move clumsily, angry at everything, short-tempered, and cruel. But I was his brother, not his lover. Marsha loved Paul, which, in this state, meant she suffered him. And so, though it deeply hurt her, she threatened to leave him.

My brother, as I have suggested, had never been particularly talkative, and the lack of that faculty, especially now, proved ominous. More importantly, had he wished to speak to anyone about this imminent crisis, it would have been Marsha, that person most resolutely denied him.

Although my family knew something was wrong— terribly wrong—with Paul, they couldn't get him to release it. My father would suggest that Paul try to unburden himself, which of course Paul could not do. My mother, for her part, would tell my father that Paul needed time, although time alone could not breach that silence that held Paul back. And sadly, beyond everything else, Paul sensed that *his* presence had caused everyone much apprehension: if my parents did not say as much, they acted as much. And Paul, like any self-respecting person, did not wish to be a millstone; he had too much pride for that.

For two weeks before Paul was to die, he had tried to talk with me about these feelings over the phone, and nothing I could say could make him feel better. Certainly, Paul could not convey how physically sick he was. When I asked him if he would like to come visit, he answered, "Yes, in a few weeks' time." Had I known that he could not physically make the trip, had I known that he would have been afraid to confront his need for alcohol, had I known a great many things, I would have driven down to the city and scooped him up. I would not have let him die.

Well, all this was with me when I decided to venture up to James Baldwin and ask him for his autograph that first meeting in 1983.

I am very uncomfortable approaching writers I respect, and for good reason. Once, when I was eighteen, I tried to meet Gwendolyn Brooks, who remains the most generous of people, and found I couldn't utter a word. Finally, after three excruciating minutes, she simply slipped the book from my hands and signed it, smiling in a way that suggested that the whole world— at least once—had acted as I had. Mortified, I had never again attempted that oceanic crossing.

Yet, seeing Baldwin, I had to make the effort. After the initial rush of well-wishers, I fell behind a lady who was thanking him "for his wonderful essays." She had five books, three posters, and two record albums, all of which Baldwin graciously autographed. Then, before I could escape, Mr. Baldwin looked up, wondering what this frazzled collection of nerve endings wanted. "Mr. Baldwin, I just want to thank you for teaching me how to think," I exclaimed in a voice that wrangled like a testy robin. I hadn't meant to say this; it was certainly the truth. Yet it seemed that such an utterance conveyed all too much, that I had resolutely, and unfairly, placed this ragtag collection of bones on Baldwin's shoulders.

After a few seconds, Baldwin, miraculously, extended his hand and said, "That's the nicest thing anyone has ever said to me. It's not true, but it's wonderful." Then he wrote "Keep on Keeping on" in my book, like the most fitting addendum to his magnificent gift of *Sonny's Blues*.

In the spring of 1985, I met Mr. Baldwin again. He was the featured speaker at the retirement celebration for Dr. James

Turner, the brilliant, zealous director of Cornell's Africana Studies and Research Center. The center, under Dr. Turner's stewardship, had survived the turbulent sixties, the arid seventies, and, at least at this writing, the sorrowful eighties. Dr. T, as his students affectionately called him, had successfully navigated the historical "time warp" that plagued my generation. We had come of age in a period of massive societal turmoil, with the Vietnam war, the Civil Rights movement, and the deaths of Dr. Martin Luther King, Malcolm X, and the Kennedys. The Africana Studies Center was the first truly *black* studies center in the nation. All of the instructors were Afro-American, Caribbean, and nonwhite; the students were primarily black and latino; for the first time at an Ivy League institution, the works of Frantz Fanon and James Baldwin were scrutinized with the respect due truly seminal thinkers. Students would study with Walter Rodney, Hoyt Fuller, and Mari Evans, to provide but a sampling of the faculty. For the record, Walter Rodney was one of the foremost theorists of Third World economic development, who would later die in a political bombing in Guyana; Hoyt Fuller was the tireless editor of *Black World* and the author of many superb essays; and Mari Evans, the poet, children's writer, and critic, possessed one of the most elegant minds in American letters. That some at Cornell did not know these distinguished pundits showed yet again the dangerous myopia that befouls academia. Indeed, the center's faculty, pound for pound, was as eminent as any department in the university.

The entire James Turner celebration was an astonishment for me. Not only would I give a joint poetry reading with Gwendolyn Brooks (and I would speak to her this time!), but I would also have the privilege of escorting James Baldwin about the campus during his brief one-night stay. Yes, this was heady stuff. And yet, before my fear could truly intensify, I was in the throes of things, picking up people at the airport, making certain that the wine had been delivered, checking the seating capacities of auditoriums.

For a marvelous two hours, James Baldwin and I were able to have a drink together. Mr. Baldwin was staying at the Sheraton Inn, which is about as bland an institution as hominy grits, and he had been awaiting me at the bar when I arrived. The bar, which resembled a slightly reworked gymnasium, had only one thing to recommend it: the booze. If the walls were full of tacky Spanish prints, the seats made of imitation leather, the whiskey could not be improved upon. Indeed, it was the only stock item in a stock paradise that one wanted, or could imagine oneself wanting. Perhaps it is the awful brutality of such prefabricated surroundings, their unmitigated banality, that makes hotel bars such perilous drinking holes: one drinks to deny the prevalent absence surrounding one, and adds one's own violence to that river of violence that will not be silenced. The bar, in this brutal economy, acts like the most cruel of mirrors: if there is little here of any value on the walls, in the seats, in the generic carpet, there can only be the self-orchestrated value that one can bring to this place—and that value, like the person slowly involved in his or her own grim calculus, would only counsel that a person flee, run out of here as quickly as he or she humanly can. That few ever make it clear of such places suggests that this algebra is a terrible one indeed.

When Baldwin saw me, he was clearly delighted, since I was someone he nominally knew. Lonely hours in a bar, in some godforsaken town, were not pleasant for anyone. But for a black person—a *famous* black person—there was always the possibility of ambush or doom. Baldwin, of all the world's writers, knew the dangers of "his American countrymen"; he had no desire to confront them anew. And thus his face—slight and boyishly animated—evidenced that at least today there would be *two* of us if they came riding.

Baldwin, unlike most people, sensed his vulnerability if not its causes. He could state that he knew he was a "faggot," and that such a proposition could cause great enmity in others. Yet he could never know the true depths of that acrimony or the desperate force which impelled him to call it forth.

104

Baldwin flaunted the aura of the famous, if he did not parody it. Effusive in word and gesture, he moved zephyrlike. His expansive hand movements, his face and eyes that angled toward the heavens as if they despaired of what lay hidden there, his brilliant elocution—all acted like a lightning rod. And yet it was not the attention of the casually interested or the mildly intoxicated that Baldwin divined; more, it was the awareness of those who had, at great peril, to bring him into their cosmos. Baldwin's presence demanded a response from those about him—and it was an injunction few welcomed.

Yet, if people routinely have trouble making room for new ideas, it is even more problematic when the novel is boisterously uncompromising. And Baldwin was certainly that. No one wrote more discerningly about human experience; and yet no one, I think, better exemplified, in all its fury and terror, life's failure to codify. Baldwin was Baldwin, plain and simple. And yet there seemed nothing more scary than this plain, simple fact. Yes, as the spiritual says, "life is revelation enough."

Still, in the Sheraton, everyone was riveted on Baldwin—doctor and mechanic alike. Neither man would wish to look like Baldwin; neither could imagine how he moved through the world; yet neither could find a way to pry his attention from him. And though some of this interest hailed from the fact that Baldwin was a "personality," there was, and very quickly, the obvious hint of hostility. Baldwin had pushed these "responsible citizens" too far; he was chaos unloosened on the American mind. Brilliant and black, rich and homosexual, outspoken and despondent, these were not the virtues that one wished to accompany that long-awaited beer. And yet, just as truthfully, no one at the bar could have known the inner Baldwin; I doubt, indeed, that many there had ever read more than a few pages of him, although I am certain his name would have triggered something—some dim recollection—in all of them.

And still it was obvious that they did sense his "secret life," or, at least, they gleaned enough about him to feel menaced and angered, which is enough—at least in Dodge City, America—to get you killed.

I recall ten years ago when I attended a memorial rally for Dr. Martin Luther King in New York City. The gathering took place in Central Park, near the boat pond, and I remember how warm it was for a January day: sunny, in the fifties, with that cold, dry brilliance that seems nature's loving gesture even toward cities. At the end of the rally, on my way across Fifth Avenue, I saw a black blind man who was obviously leaving the celebration. He looked lost, and yet I wasn't certain that he wanted my help. After a few moments, I introduced myself and asked if he would like to take my arm. The thing I most remember, the thing that ranks as one of the greatest astonishments of my life, was that as we walked, the blind man kept talking about the racial injustices of this country. Now, this man had never seen; he had been sightless since birth. And yet he knew he was black; he knew that his skin color meant a rigidly limited life; and he was angry. I learned, I guess then, that life conveys truth in miraculous ways, and that these men in the bar—however abstrusely—might well know something about Baldwin.

One of them, with a few more drinks and fewer inhibitions, boisterously pointed out to his high-minded friend that there was a "fruit" sitting at the next table, by which he meant Baldwin. And I saw Baldwin smiling at that—a smile as self-possessed, loud, and defiant as Zeus's torch. Suddenly I realized Baldwin was dangerous: dangerous because he would not give in or acquiesce; dangerous because, come hell or murder, he would not permit anyone the salve of silence. *Come take me*, he seemed to say; *I'm not afraid, are you?*

And then I sensed, as if a subway had struck me, that if Baldwin looked again at the table, the drunk man would have cause to fight. Indeed, possibly the whole bar might rise up like an ocean, the air seemed so pregnant, so volatile. Luckily, the liquor was still a puzzle to the drunk; he had yet to find his legs. That his mouth worked, at least at this moment, was a wondrous apparition. The drunk, inchoately, for five or six minutes, was still slobbering something, wheezing much like a rusty hinge. I hoped, at least now, he was no longer talking about Baldwin, since in his navigations he could be onto anything, be it roses or swampfire, his loved or loveless nights; I hoped also, because I *too* was there, that he wasn't talking about me.

Thankfully, after a few more looks and some faltering conversation, Baldwin seemed satisfied. "I should leap up and kiss him," Baldwin said. And God, I hoped he would not.

Baldwin and I talked a good bit about writing, especially about his essays. I asked him about "Stranger in the Village," which I rank as the finest discussion of the American racial scene, even though it was written some thirty years ago. I wanted to know how long it had taken him to compose it. To my surprise, he was enormously candid. "Stranger" had taken eight weeks to write—and Baldwin wrote hard, ten-to-twelve-hour days, with little sleep and much booze. He had carried it about with him for six months, in Switzerland and Paris, feeling "no one would be interested in it."

It seemed a long jump from the writer before me—author of eighteen works, *successful*, if that is the word—and that terribly prose-laden lad, with the powerful essay burning in his pocket. And yet his disarming candor, his lack, at least here, of a discernible public presence, convinced me that the man and the doubt-infested lad held legitimate claim on the person sitting before me.

In all honesty, I was somewhat uncomfortable in Baldwin's presence. To me he was America's greatest living writer; he had taught me how to think, and his rhetorical structures had invigorated my own small essays. Yet I was worried—and I feel even now ashamed to state it—that he might make a pass at me. This, I must admit, was not without cause: many of my friends had warned me of the possibility; Baldwin, indeed, had come on to some of them.

Still, if my response made no sense, my own dissonance haunted the air. Intellectually, I knew better: I was not stupid. Should such a situation arise, I would simply say no. But

107

the real tragedy was that I squandered what precious little time I had with this genius, worrying about something so self-crippling, so idiotic. And yet, and I must be truthful, I could think of little else but envisioning possible scenarios and my escape. It is one thing to state that one is not homophobic or racist (talk is cheap), but the fear—dark, irrational, problematic—must be confronted; and in that confrontation, I had far more in common with that brutal, coarse drunk than I would like to admit. (Some of you out there, I know, will be yelling: "McClane, you *should* know better. Stop being homophobic." And I will answer that I *do* know better, but knowledge has little to do with fear. Indeed, if it did, no one who drives an automobile would logically be afraid to fly, since the chances of an airplane mishap are minuscule in comparison to the possibility of an accident on the highway. And yet tell that to the man whose heart races like a hummingbird's wings at the thought of a whirling propeller; tell it to him as he sees the cockpit turn into a plastic funeral pyre, the incinerated bodies curdling at the windows like roasted ticks; tell it to him as he sees his own arms dangling out the scar in the wing, like the stewardess in James Dickey's terrifying poem "Falling." Tell it to him. Speak logically. Cogently.)

Baldwin, of course, has written masterfully about America's fear of difference. It was he who reminded us that we as Americans are ahistorical, that our lack of a self-critical connection to history—and to each other—has made us dangerously simplistic, patently moralistic, and socially irrelevant. Indeed, as Baldwin asserts, the world we face today has no relationship to the world we imagine: the so-called Third World *exists*, and not as some exotic ragtag carpet bazaar but as the real province of three-quarters of the world's people: people who love their children, who work, and who make love, if they have the time. Incontestably, most of the world's people do not have the luxury of profaning others; their adventure has demanded a historical *precision*, the lack of which can only further confuse and condemn us. Sadly, as Baldwin reminds us, Ameri-

cans still believe that they have the possibility for innocence—
a notion as historically delusional as our penchant to offer
oxymoronic statements such as "war for peace." As Baldwin
painfully said to me at the Sheraton, "One wonders if the world
can survive America."

The last time I saw James Arthur Baldwin was at his
memorial service at the Cathedral of St. John the Divine. I was
there, with so many others, because I wanted to celebrate someone who had so wonderfully celebrated me.

The memorial service was a difficult congress. A public remembrance—for Baldwin belonged to the world—it was
also a funeral (a last farewell for his family), and the confluence
of both was far from easy. I recall, while watching Baldwin's
family come in, that many of them seemed astonished at the
presence of so many onlookers: grief is a private matter; and it
was their Jimmy who was gone. The realization that "Jimmy"
was also mourned by untold hundreds was important, yes; but at
this moment—this *final* moment—one's grief was too pointed,
too in need of an object, a reason, a primacy. So, even at this
ultimate juncture, Baldwin was again being taken from them:
yes, here was the world, intrusive as always.

The service was profoundly moving, with Olatunji's
funeral drums, passionate statements from Imamu Baraka, Maya
Angelou, and Toni Morrison, and the hundreds of desperate
self-contained expressions of grief. I was heartened by the out-
pouring of community; I saw the literati—which I expected—
and the well-dressed professionals, but I also witnessed numbers of street youth, many wearing dungaree jackets and sneak-
ers, some coming into the Lord's house, I trust, for only this one
time. These were all Baldwin's people, and he would have been
pleased.

Yet I also felt a tremendous sense of anger when I heard
Olatunji's final funeral oration—the "Continuum Drums"—which
is as dolorous a piece of music as the world has ever witnessed.
This lovely elegy had once been mine; I had once been African.

109

Yet it was only at the death of Baldwin—someone who learned to love Africa, as we all would have to learn to love ourselves—that I could intuit the perimeters of my loss. *Nothing is ever escaped*, Baldwin wrote. *Nothing is ever escaped.*

I would like to state at this writing that I will never be afraid, small-minded, or despicable again, but I know my Baldwin too well. As he reminded me at the Sheraton, "The most difficult thing is to say yes to life—after you've hurt people, after you've understood how much you can soil the world."

It is that soiled body that I, and all of us, confront every day; the same soiled body that both loved and failed my brother; the same soiled body that Baldwin, in his final words to me in Ithaca, graciously wished peace.

I remember how odd I looked when Baldwin said that to me, both amused that after our wonderful conversation we would ultimately be relegated to cliché, and also mindful that the world provides this common banter because so much of life remains the inevitable, unremarkable, unalterable chain of despair.

Looking pleased and then thoughtful, Baldwin caught my drift and broadly smiled. "Peace and love," he reiterated, this time thinning the air with his hands. "Don't forget, Ken, they're real words; we have only to make them serviceable." And then Baldwin walked slowly to the table where the drunk had hurled his invectives, and smiled again, looking very tenderly at the man who, now asleep, appeared much like a beached whale.

Between Yes and No

When they came in and said that if we stayed we
would be officially arrested, I decided to stay. I
decided to stay and accept punishment and a police
record not only because I thought it was important
for us to maintain our stand, but because at that
moment I was questioning the fundamental
principles of this University that would condone
apartheid and oppression in South Africa by
maintaining their investments, and punish us for
our freedom to speak against them.

—Kristin Bole, a Cornell student,
in testimony before the University
Hearing Board on May 4, 1985

Recently I was a willful spectator at a "shanty raising"
by a large contingent of Cornell faculty members—some ninety
or so spirited souls. I say willful because I *willed* myself to be
inactive, but I am getting ahead of myself. The haphazard
structure—three-quarters good intentions and much architec-
tural luck—symbolized the faculty's protest against Cornell's
continued investment in South Africa, and their further outrage
against a university-imposed court injunction which, in its far-
ranging legal implications, effectively stifled all manner of
campus dissent.

The faculty shanty, however bedraggled, was in direct
opposition to a university prohibition. With hammer and nail,
the faculty were demonstrating their support for students who
had previously erected numerous "outlawed" shanties, only to

find themselves arrested, their shanties torn down. More importantly, the faculty members—after great debate and much fear—
were finally placing themselves, and their jobs, in jeopardy. No
longer could the faculty condone the wanton arrest of their best
and most humanitarian students. As one faculty member stated,
"At Cornell, we used to award degrees; now it is court appearance tickets."

As a rule, university faculty do not act precipitously.
Professors always have reasons—*good* ones—for further consid-
eration and debate. In this case, the university could arrest the
"shanty builders" for criminal trespass (a felony in New York
State), since the participants would be violating a New York
State court order; or Cornell could, citing precedent, move for
their immediate dismissal from university employment. Both
options, of course, were considered highly unlikely; ninety
distinguished faculty members is no insignificant number.

Yet for people who spend their lives probing the seemingly minuscule for the cosmic, the stakes were high. One
professor, although he strongly agreed with the faculty's decision
to build the shanty, could not bring himself to face the possibility
of another arrest. Incarcerated for six years in Chile, he had lost
his hearing in his left ear from police torture. He wanted to help
(he knew, as few others do, the horrors of state-sanctioned
oppression), but the *fear*—like the hot wire formerly stabbed in
his left ear lobe—would not go away.

That the ninety faculty members undertook to build a
shanty evidenced their profound disillusionment in the Cornell
administration. It is an "especial evil" that can get five faculty
members to agree, not to mention ninety variously impassioned
souls. Yet, clearly, it was the horror of watching nonviolent
students routinely arrested, seeing their dreams turned belly-up
by contemptible, cynical old men, that so angered everyone.
Kristin Bole, cited above, was certainly indicative of the student
protesters. The administration might talk about "reasoned debate"
and "moral character," but it was quick to summon the police;
the demonstrators, with their minds and their lives, were *evidenc-*

ing moral integrity. The university president might preach about the horrors of apartheid: he might even *believe* his words; yet, as in Soweto, he was quick to send the dissident to jail.

The proscriptive injunction had been handed down by a New York State Supreme Court justice in the spring of 1985, when the university faced repeated acts of mass civil disobedience at Day Hall, the administration building. During the two months of peaceful sit-ins, the university had arrested more than sixteen hundred students, faculty, and staff—the largest tally of arrestees ever recorded at an American educational institution. In fact, Cornell, incredibly, had arrested more than one-tenth of its total constituency, making arrest, as someone joked, "Cornell's largest major."

I should describe how these protests occurred. At about three P.M. each day, hundreds of divestment protesters would congregate in the halls of the administration building and form two orderly columns on either side of the hallway, permitting people to pass. The demonstrators—often studying, sometimes talking quietly—would remain until five P.M., when a university official, most often the dean of students, would ask them to leave, declaring that Day Hall officially closed at five. At five-fifteen P.M. the dean would inform the students that they were now in violation of "The Campus Code of Conduct," which prohibits the unauthorized use of university property. The dean would then tell the students that they would be arrested if they continued to remain. Inevitably, the students would continue sitting, the campus police would be called in, and the demonstrators would either peacefully walk out of the building with the arresting officer or they would be carried out. In these confrontations the students were always nonviolent; the police, until one terrible Monday, were always the epitome of self-control and discipline.

Understandably, in the daily arrests, the students and the campus police developed an odd intimacy. The police and the students saw each other for two hours in Day Hall, and often for three more hours while summonses were issued. In the long hours of arrests, and the longer hours of issuing court appearance tickets, the police and the demonstrators were forced together; the administration, however, was never in evidence. Like Greek gods, the administration gave orders, they pulled the strings, but they remained comfortably invisible.

In seeking the injunction "banning all political meetings and shanty building," the Cornell administration maintained that such large-scale divestment protests made it impossible for the institution to function and that, because of the unprecedented nature of mass arrests, Cornell could no longer ensure the safety of the demonstrators or university personnel. Yet the judge—a Cornell alumnus—never questioned why the university had created its own dilemma; clearly the protesters had not arrested themselves. Nor did he pursue substantive questions concerning the demonstrators' alleged acts of "willful violence," which the university so relentlessly contended.

In truth, the demonstrators were idealistic students, need I say kids, who believed that Cornell should not profane its educational mission by profiting from apartheid. They were not, as the university argued, "anarchists" or "thugs." I was present at every demonstration; the judge and the university administration were not. These students neither damaged property nor threatened anyone. After their daily sit-in, they would diligently clean up Day Hall, removing all trash, leaflets, and the like. In fact, Day Hall became so tidy that one of the regular custodians quipped, "These kids may make me lose my job."

Indeed, when a campus patrolman, Officer Newby, collapsed from exhaustion while carrying out one of the demonstrators who had gone "limp" in the classic passive-resistance tactic, the student protesters became disconsolate. Realizing that the campus police were merely workers and not the targets of their protest, the students quickly decided to walk out of the administration building, thereby ending any possibility for further mishap; quietly, the next day, these same students presented Officer Newby's wife with three hundred dollars to aid in his recuperation. These students were not hooligans; they were saints. Even *The Syracuse Herald American*, hardly a hotbed of liberalism, chanced to write that the divestment advocates were "characteristically gentle and humane."

Yet still the Cornell administration resolutely brought out the cannons; and one wondered, when looking at the bright-faced, chaplainlike students, what indeed had transpired to so countervail good sense.

The first faculty shanty took about two hours to construct: academics are not good with their hands, and theory, in itself, does not a shanty make. Predictably, there were two speeches: one by an African philosopher, who spoke as eloquently as one humanly could; and another by Phil Lewis, a professor of romance studies, who recounted the university's litany of misrepresentations and acts of bad faith.

I had participated in many of the events narrated by Professor Lewis, and I recalled, with particular bitterness, the four-day discussions with the Cornell provost, which I had instigated. I had proposed these talks after a particularly frightening encounter—on a terribly humid Monday—when the campus police, understandably tired, lost their cool and nearly bludgeoned a group of students. The police had been working overtime for many days—many of them had not had a day off in nearly a month—and they had just returned from a training program at the firing range to learn, yet again, that students had reoccupied the administration building. Seeing these officers not dressed in their usual attire, but in army fatigues, recalled a time I had desperately tried to forget—a time when I had watched American troops, clubs in hand, move briskly through groups of young college demonstrators, flailing at their prostrate bodies, as if they were mere husks of wheat. In their army garb, I realized, the campus police were *soldiers*—that is, that they had a *cause* and a *gun,* and their cause, at least today, was not mine.

Indeed, as their new uniforms suggested a new equation to me, so too did they corroborate a new reality for them. On a good day, the campus police could remember that these were mere *students* who had kept them away from their families and

115

who made it "impossible to cut the lawn"; but today, this generosity, like their usual attire, was not in evidence. Today, they were hot, tired, and cranky; today, they felt, for the first time, that these demonstrations might go on forever.

So, when the students, for some unknown reason, congregated a stone's throw from their usual protest position in Day Hall, the campus police began brandishing their clubs. For the first time I saw something in the patrolmen's eyes I had not seen before. It was that look of bottomless fatigue and resignation, that look which reminds us that human beings can only endure so much, and pushed beyond that can do the unthinkable.

These patrolmen were not bad men, or weak, or slovenly; in fact, they were quite honorable. To this date, the campus police had performed valiantly as peace officers: they had treated the students with respect, kindness, and inordinate charity. But such extreme selflessness cannot be tendered forever: *human beings remain human beings.* These policemen had been placed in an untenable position, in which they were supposed to hold back an uncontainable flood. Every day the protesters kept coming; every day there were more people to be carried, and more weariness.

No one should be asked to do this. The administration, certainly, was never present in the midday heat or in the dark hours; they were not missing their families day in and day out. It was William Faulkner who argued, most beautifully, "for human appreciation for what humans are." Indeed, for Cornell to fail to recognize these officers' all-too-human vulnerability was the greatest act of bureaucratic inhumanity. It was, in fact, criminal—as criminal as testing the atomic bomb, in 1945, three miles from troops deployed in foxholes.

In an attempt to defuse the ever-palpable risk of violence, I proposed a meeting between the senior administration and the divestment protesters. My plan was simple. I hoped to convince the administration that the students' protest fell within the broad perimeters of "symbolic" speech, that civil disobedience or shanty building is a First Amendment right, something any educational community is obligated to respect. I had also hoped—but of this I harbored few illusions—that the administration might even embrace these students, seeing in their selflessness something of great moral provender. But, at bottom, I would have been content to have the administration affirm our *right* to protest.

When I approached the students with my idea for an upper-level meeting, they reluctantly consented, expressing little faith in the provost's goodwill. I countered that inasmuch as the provost had been in China during much of the demonstrations, he might not have "the crippling mental baggage" of his colleagues; and might even, God knows, have the wherewithal to deny the Orwellian universe which now so engulfed us. I argued here, I must confess, more for myself than for them: I could not bear to see anyone hurt; I loved this university and its students. I had spent fifteen years here as an undergraduate, a graduate student, and now a faculty member, and it had been my lifeblood. The students, I think, perceived my ambivalence, even if I myself did not. Still, the possibility that any action might avert human injury easily carried the day.

The provost's meetings were a sham. On the first day of our deliberations, the provost floated a proposal involving the number of shanties the administration would permit that was infinitely more generous than the one he would present on the last day of our deliberations: no shanties at all.

The provost, like most of us, worked for someone. Although he did come into our meetings with a perspective that was initially neutral, his administrative side quickly reasserted itself. If we held his attention for four days, the president held his future. And no matter how much we swayed him—and I trust, at least from his intense interest in the students, we swayed him a great deal—our announcements were too frightening and too exhortative to be embraced. To hear us, the provost would have had to forswear safety. And as James Baldwin cautions, *To act is to be committed and to be committed is to be in danger.* Sadly, the provost was no pioneer.

117

Understandably, I felt enormously betrayed and angry. I had beseeched the protesters to come to the table; it was their trust in me that the provost had profaned. All of us had spent four long days and nights trying to reach a consensus—indeed, it looked as if we might save face for all concerned. And then that embarrassing last-minute debacle. It is understandable, in a vexatious situation, when people fail to reach an agreement: agreement in the best of worlds is problematic. Yet when one party acts in bad faith, it makes a mockery of the terribly profound and difficult orchestrations toward community. It is one thing to fail, however unfortunate; it is another willingly to corrupt. The university had, for whatever its twisted reasons, abused our good intentions. And these were students, kids, people who wanted to make the world a better place, who saw inhumanity anywhere as their rightful concern. Students should dream; universities, I used to believe, celebrated what was *best* in us, and not our horror, our avarice, our villainy.

These thoughts pressed in on me as I heard the last few phrases of Professor Lewis's speech, punctuated every so often by the dull sound of hammering nails. The faculty shanty was a good one. I had watched it take shape, and had even unloaded some of its curious makings: awkward-shaped pieces of plywood, poster board, and cardboard. No matter how miserable its undergirding, this shanty was still far more sturdy, at least in its materials, than was its South African prototype. American rubbish is lavish compared to that of most of the world; and this thought—like a note one suddenly unearths in a familiar passage of music—quickly became omnipresent. Invariably, one's *Americanness* always seems to haunt one; and inevitably, the search to find a place where it might be otherwise is a profoundly *American* quest.

Quickly, the one shanty had grown to two, and all of the members of the faculty, it seemed, had taken up the symbolic hammer. The structure somehow held, although I will never forget Professor James Turner shouting for a pole or "something to keep the roof up." Someone eminently resourceful finally found a suitable buttress, and the roof, though sagging, looked at least tenable. A few more nails, a touch here and there of cardboard, and the shanty would be finished.

I had painfully watched this evolution, but not with the eye to ridicule so evident among some of the spectators. Two students to my left kept commenting on the professors' clothing, while another smugly offered, "I wish they'd do their work, and publish some articles." I tried not to listen; I tried not to strangle them. Such noise, however parochial, seems forever to get my goat; indeed, if I have thirty students who admire my lectures, it is the one dissenting voice, the one who states that I am too rambling or too romantic, who earns my notice.

Still, despite these nay-sayers, I had wanted to help construct the shanty. Apartheid, double-dealing, and institutional invective had no place in my university. I had seen what it had done to all of us. Recently, a white student had been hit by a rock and had been called a "nigger lover" because she chose to live in a predominantly black dorm; then, a few days later, a white woman falsely claimed that she had been raped by a black man, only to confess later that the entire thing had been a hoax. I submit that these events—however unfortunate and inevitable— were further exacerbated by a climate in which moral confusion reigned. Apartheid, like any cancer, taints everything it touches. All of us, no matter what our beliefs, had been infected. Friends had become oddly distant; conversations often became dull or silly; and the *real* talk—the essential, hard, perilous getting-it-said—became too dangerous, too precipitous. Of course, this is tragic wherever in life it occurs; but in a university community, where meaning is, at bottom, all we have, it is nefarious.

Still, no matter how much I wanted to participate, I held myself in check. For, as luck would have it, I had recently been appointed to the University Hearing Board, whose job it was to adjudicate cases involving breaches of university regulations, such as shanty building. Insomuch as I was one of the few confirmed leftists on the twenty-four-member panel (all of whom, incidentally, were appointed by the administration), it

119

behooved me—both strategically and politically—to conduct myself above reproach. The hearing board is no impotent gathering of old men. It can expel students, recommend dismissal of faculty, and mandate change in university policy. Indeed, it was only the sweeping fiat of the board which so held my feet. For, as I kept reminding myself, it might well be these same hammering faculty members that I (and hopefully a few others) might be called upon to save. And so, with much difficulty, I held my place.

After an impromptu verse of "We Shall Overcome," a makeshift cardboard door was finally fitted to the shanty, and everyone seemed oddly joyous. I hadn't yet lost my conviction to remain a bystander, and the campus police, at least, had not yet moved on the faculty. Suddenly, out of nowhere, a television camera was pressed in my face, and the interviewer—a tough-looking blond woman—asked me what I felt "watching the Cornell faculty build a shanty." I thought long and hard about the question, remembering the distinct dangers of television, and mentally prepared an answer that could not be edited or misunderstood. Looking straight into the camera, I stated, "As a Cornell faculty member I respect and admire the faculty's action. They bring honor to their calling and to the institution." The woman smiled as the camera drew in closer, and I sensed, for the first time, that there was a person beneath that rough exterior. Then, as I attempted to walk away, I heard her ask, "If you feel that way, why didn't you help build the shanty?"

Time seemed to slow; I felt as if I had entered a deep cave. The two long years of antiapartheid protests; the hundreds of arrests; the fear I felt as I was arrested two years before, my crazy desire to grab the patrolman's gun, because he was white and I was black and scared; the dismal provost's meetings; the University Hearing Board nomination; the students and their great courage—all of this flashed before me, when, incredibly, although I felt myself walking over the edge, I heard myself answering, "I did. I *did*."

Books in the African American Life Series

*Coleman Young and Detroit Politics:
    From Social Activist to Power
    Broker,* by Wilbur Rich, 1988

*Great Black Russian: A Novel on the
    Life and Times of Alexander
    Pushkin,* by John Oliver Killens,
    1989

*Indignant Heart: A Black Worker's
    Journal,* by Charles Denby, 1989
    (reprint)

The Spook Who Sat by the Door, by
    Sam Greenlee, 1989 (reprint)

*Roots of African American Drama: An
    Anthology of Early Plays,
    1858–1938,* edited by Leo
    Hamalian and James V. Hatch,
    1990

*Voices of the Self: A Study of Language
    Competence,* by Keith Gilyard,
    1991

Walls: Essays, 1985–1990, by Kenneth
    McClane, 1991